Integrated Korean
Intermediate 1

KLEAR Textbooks in Korean Language

Integrated Korean

Intermediate 1

Second Edition

Young-mee Cho   Hyo Sang Lee   Carol Schulz   Ho-min Sohn   Sung-Ock Sohn

University of Hawai'i Press
Honolulu

This textbook series has been developed by the Korean Language Education and Research Center (KLEAR) with the support of the Korea Foundation.

Library of Congress Cataloging-in-Publication Data
Integrated Korean : intermediate 1 / Young-mee Cho... [et al.].
        p. cm.—(KLEAR textbooks in Korean language)
        ISBN 978-0-8248-2418-1 (cloth : alk. paper)—ISBN 978-0-8248-2419-8
(pbk. alk. paper)
        1. Korean language—Textbooks for foreign speakers—English. I. Cho,
Young-mee. II. Series.
PL913.I5812 2001
495.7'82421—dc21

                                                00-033782

Integrated Korean: Intermediate 1, **Second** Edition
ISBN 978-0-8248-3650-4 (pbk. alk. paper)

Illustrations and photos by Sejin Han

Audio files for this volume may be downloaded on the Web in MP3 format at
http://www.kleartextbook.com

A set of accompanying audio CDs for this book is also available for purchase. For
more information, contact:
Order Department
University of Hawai`i Press
2840 Kolowalu Street
Honolulu, Hawaii 96822
Toll free: 888-847-7377
Outside North America: 808-956-8255

Camera-ready copy has been provided by the authors.

Printed by Sheridan Books, Inc.

Contents

Preface to the Second Edition

The inaugural volumes of *Integrated Korean*, Intermediate 1 and 2, of the Korean Language Education & Research Center (KLEAR) appeared in 2001, followed in subsequent years by upper-level (Advanced Intermediate, Advanced, and High Advanced) volumes. The IK series, especially the beginning and intermediate volumes, has attracted a large number of learners of Korean around the world, especially in the United States and other English-speaking countries.

Currently, more than seventy universities and colleges are using the books for regular classroom instruction. The IK series has been popular particularly because the authors endeavored to develop all volumes in accordance with performance-based principles and methodology—contextualization, learner-centeredness, use of authentic materials, usage-orientedness, balance between acquiring and using skills, and integration of speaking, listening, reading, writing, and culture. Also, grammar points were systematically introduced with simple but adequate explanations and abundant examples and exercises.

The volumes, however, are not free from minor shortcomings that call for improvement. While using the volumes, classroom teachers and students of keen insight, as well as the authors themselves, have noticed such weaknesses here and there. The authors have felt that the volumes should be updated to better reflect the current needs of students. Consequently, at the original authors' recommendation, a revision team was formed. It consisted of

Mee-Jeong Park, University of Hawai'i at Mānoa (Coordinator)
Sang-suk Oh, Harvard University
Joowon Suh, Princeton University
Mary Shin Kim, University of Hawai'i at Mānoa

With a strong commitment to offering the best possible learning opportunities, the revision team has painstakingly reorganized and restructured the material in this second edition of the textbook based on feedback received from an extensive survey. This revised edition includes a new layout that more closely mimics the actual classroom environment, making it easier and more intuitive for both teacher and student. Both

Intermediate 1 and Intermediate 2 now consist of more lessons, but each lesson is more focused, with fewer grammar patterns, and each of these lessons is now divided into two main sections—Conversation 1 and Conversation 2 (each with its own vocabulary list)—followed by Narration. There are more exercises that focus on vocabulary and grammar, with all exercises following our new goal of clarification and intuitiveness.

Each situation/topic-based lesson of the main texts consists of model dialogues, narration, new words and expressions, vocabulary notes, culture, grammar, usage to cover pragmatic uses, and English translation of dialogues. In response to comments from hundreds of students and instructors of the first edition, this new edition features a more attractive two-color design with all new photos and illustrations, additional lessons, and vocabulary exercises.

On behalf of KLEAR and the original authors of IK Intermediate 1 and 2, I wholeheartedly thank the revision team for their indefatigable efforts and devotion.

Ho-min Sohn
KLEAR President
July 2011

Objectives

Lesson 1 날씨와 계절 [Weather and Seasons]

Texts	Grammar
Conversation 1 어느 계절을 제일 좋아하세요?	1. Change of state: A.S.~어/아지다 'become, get to be' 2. Sentence ending ~잖아요. 'You know, . . .' (assuming agreement)
Conversation 2 날씨가 추워졌네요.	3. Noun-modifying form ~던 (retrospective) 4. V.S.~(으)ㄴ 다음에/후에 'after doing (something)' 5. Expressing speaker's wish: ~(으)면 좋겠다
Narration 일기예보	
Culture	**Usage**
음력과 양력: The use of the lunar and solar (Gregorian) calendars	1. Describing weather 2. Indicating possibility and capability 3. Listening to weather forecasts

Lesson 2 옷과 유행 [Clothing and Fashion]

Texts	Grammar
Conversation 1 백화점에서 옷을 사려고 해요.	1. V.S.~(으)려고 'intending to'; V.S.~(으)려고 하다 'intend to' 2. V.S.~기(가) 쉽다/어렵다 'it is easy/difficult to . . .'
Conversation 2 요즘 짧은 치마가 유행이에요.	3. N1말고 N2 'not N1 but N2' 4. Expressions of permission and prohibition: V.S. ~어도/아도 되다; V.S.~(으)면 안 되다 5. ~(으)ㄴ/는/(으)ㄹ 것 같다 'it seems/looks like'
Narration 백화점 쇼핑	
Culture	**Usage**
한국의 의(衣)생활: The Korean life pertaining to clothes	1. Requesting, granting, and denying permission 2. Making plans 3. Describing physical appearance 4. Shopping

Lesson 3 여행 [Travel]	
Texts	**Grammar**
Conversation 1 한국에 가게 됐어요.	1. ~게 되다: change or turn of events 2. ~(으)면 되다 'have only to . . .', 'All one needs is . . .'
Conversation 2 한국에 갔다 왔어요.	3. Doubling of ~었-: ~었었-/~았었-/~ㅆ었- 4. ~어/아 본 적(이) 있다/없다 'There has been an/no occasion of . . .' 5. ~(으)니까: expressing a reason or logical sequence
Narration 소피아의 한국 여행	
Culture	**Usage**
경주: The ancient capital of the Silla Kingdom	1. Calling a travel agency and buying an airline ticket 2. Talking about vacation and summer jobs 3. Describing past events 4. Skimming newspaper ads for airline tickets and travel information

Lesson 4 한국 생활 I [Life in Korea I]	
Texts	**Grammar**
Conversation 1 인사동에 가는 길이에요.	1. ~는 길이다/~는 길에 '(be) on one's way' 2. ~거든요. 'You see, (because)~'
Conversation 2 소포를 부치려고 하는데요.	3. N(이)요. 'It is [noun]' 4. ~(으)려면 'if . . . intends to do' 5. ~어야/아야지요. 'definitely/indeed/surely should/ought to/have to'
Narration 우진이의 편지	
Culture	**Usage**
인사동	1. Using postal services 2. Giving a warning and seeking advice 3. Writing personal letters

Lesson 5 한국 생활 II [Life in Korea II]	
Texts	**Grammar**
Conversation 1 방값도 싸고 괜찮아.	1. The intimate speech style ~어/아 2. ~(으)ㄴ/는 편이다 'It is more the case of . . . than the other.' 3. ~(으)ㄴ/는지 알다/모르다 'know/don't know whether (what, who, where, when) . . .'

Conversation 2 이사 온 지 얼마나 됐어요?	4. A: ~(으)ㄴ 지 얼마나 됐어요? 'How long has it been since . . .?' B: ~(으)ㄴ 지 TIME SPAN(이/가) 됐어요. 'It has been . . . since . . .' 5. ~다가: transference of an action/state to another
Narration 스티브의 하숙방	
Culture	**Usage**
하숙과 자취	1. Searching for housing 2. Describing buildings and interiors 3. Initiating a conversation and introducing oneself 4. Giving compliments and responding to compliments

Lesson 6 대중 교통 [Public Transportation]

Texts	**Grammar**
Conversation 1 등산 갈 준비 다 됐니?	1. The plain style ~(는/ㄴ)다 2. The use of the plain style in speaking 3. V.S.~기로 하다 'plan to/decide to'
Conversation 2 관악산 입구까지 가 주세요.	4. Indirect quotation: ~다고 하다, ~(으/느)냐고 하다, ~(으)라고 하다, ~자고 하다 5. 아무리 ~어도/아도 'no matter how . . .'
Narration 스티브의 일기	
Culture	**Usage**
주민등록증	1. Asking for and giving directions 2. Using public transportation 3. Making telephone calls 4. Writing a journal

Lesson 7 가게에서 [At a Store]

Texts	**Grammar**
Conversation 1 사과 한 상자에 얼마예요?	1. ~어/아 보이다 'someone/something appears . . ./ looks . . .' 2. Passive verbs 3. ~어/아 있다 'In the state of being . . .'
Conversation 2 여기 뭐 사러 왔어?	4. ~어/아 가지고 'because, since'; 'by doing/being' 5. ~는 데(에) 'in/for ~ing . . .'
Narration 동네 시장	
Culture	**Usage**
택배	1. Talking about food and making a shopping list 2. Making recipes 3. Expressing hesitation

1과 날씨와 계절 [Weather and Seasons]

| Conversation 1 | 어느 계절을 제일 좋아하세요? |

(민지와 마크가 도서관 앞에서 이야기하고 있습니다.)

민지: 날씨가 많이 시원해졌지요?[G1.1]

마크: 네, 정말 시원해졌어요. 여름이 끝나고
        벌써 가을이 됐네요. 올해 여름은 장마가
        유난히 길어서 지겨웠어요.

민지: 마크 씨는 어느 계절을 제일 좋아하세요?

마크: 저는 봄이 제일 좋아요. 날씨도 따뜻하고,
        꽃도 많이 피잖아요.[G1.2] 민지 씨는요?

민지: 저는 스키도 탈 수 있고 방학도 길어서
        겨울이 더 좋아요.

마크: 아, 그래요? 그럼, 민지 씨는 겨울이
        기다려지겠네요.

민지: 네, 그렇지만
        단풍 구경을
        할 수 있어서
        가을도 좋아해요.

참, 마크 씨, 10월에 설악산에 단풍 구경하러
가는데 같이 안 갈래요?

마크: 단풍 구경이요? 그렇지 않아도 가 보고
싶었는데 잘 됐네요.

COMPREHENSION QUESTIONS

1. 지금은 어느 계절입니까?
2. 마크는 왜 봄을 제일 좋아합니까?
3. 겨울 방학이 깁니까, 여름 방학이 깁니까?
4. 민지는 왜 가을과 겨울을 좋아합니까?
5. 민지는 10월에 무엇을 하고 싶어합니까?

NEW WORDS

NOUN		VERB	
공기	air	기다려지다	to be wished
구름	cloud	(구름이) 끼다	to get cloudy
기온	temperature	낮아지다	to get lower
낮	daytime	내려가다	to go down
단풍	fall foliage	되다	②to function, work
런던	London	시원해지다	to become cooler
설악산	Seorak Mount	피다	to bloom
스파게티	spaghetti	**ADJECTIVE**	
야외	the outside	낮다	to be low
에어컨	air conditioner	맑다	to be clear
외국어	foreign language	지겹다	to be boring
유럽	Europe	**ADVERB**	
음식값	food cost	계속	continuously
장마	rainy season	벌써	already
전화비	phone bill	유난히	particularly
콘서트	concert	**SUFFIX**	
하늘	sky	~잖아요	you know
		~어/아지다	to become

NEW EXPRESSIONS

1. 시원하다 has a range of meanings from 'to be cool in temperature, be refreshing, inspiring' to 'to be pleasing and satisfying.' That is why this adjective can be used not only to describe cold water (시원한 물) but also to express the feeling of satisfaction when drinking hot tea or taking a warm bath. Some examples are shown below:

시원한 바람	a cool, refreshing breeze
시원한 주스	a cool, refreshing juice
숙제를 다 해서 시원하다.	A load is off my mind after I finish my homework.
시원하게 말하다	to get right to the point

2. The month of October is often written with an Arabic number as in 10월. It is spelled and pronounced as 시월 and not 십월.

3. 잘 됐네요.　　　That's great, that's good news (it turned out well).
　마침 잘 됐네요.　That's great (it turned out well) just in time.

GRAMMAR

G1.1　Change of state: A.S.~어/아지다 'become, get to be'

Examples

(1)　A:　벌써 겨울이네요.
　　　B:　감기 조심하세요. 이번 주부터 날씨가 추**워져요**.

(2)　A:　방이 참 깨끗**해졌네요.**
　　　B:　너무 더러워서 오랜만에 청소 좀 했어요.

(3)　A:　요즘 런던 날씨가 어때요?
　　　B:　계속 구름이 껴 있었는데 주말부터 맑**아질** 거예요.

(4)　A:　서울에 차가 참 많**아졌지요?**
　　　B:　네, 정말 운전하기 힘들**어졌어요.**

(5)　　A:　　오늘 서울 날씨가 어때요?
　　　　B:　　기온이 많이 낮**아졌어요**.

Notes

1. This construction, attached to an adjective stem (A.S.), expresses a change from one state or condition to another. This construction changes an adjective into a verb.

2. The adjective in this construction denotes the resulting state or condition, as in 봄에는 날씨가 따뜻해져요 'In spring, the weather becomes warmer.' If a present state is a result of a change in the past, the past tense form is used, as in 이제 깨끗해졌어요 'It's now become clean.'

3. The following table shows the conjugation patterns.

ㅂ irregular	춥다	추워지다
	덥다	더워지다
ㅡ irregular	바쁘다	바빠지다
	예쁘다	예뻐지다
ㄹ irregular	멀다	멀어지다
	길다	길어지다
르 irregular	빠르다	빨라지다
	다르다	달라지다
하다	깨끗하다	깨끗해지다

Exercises

1. Change the following sentences using ~어/아지다.

　　(1)　　동생이 (예쁘다).　　　　동생이 예뻐졌어요.
　　(2)　　여름에는 낮이 (길다).　　_____
　　(3)　　날씨가 (흐리다).　　　　_____
　　(4)　　시험이 (어렵다).　　　　_____

(5)   기온이 (낮다).   _____

(6)   시험이 끝나서 시간이 (많다). _____

(7)   하늘이 (맑다).   _____

2. Give an appropriate response in the following situations.

(1)   여름이 되었어요.   날씨가 더워졌어요.

(2)   대학교 4학년이 되었어요.   _____

(3)   친구를 오래간만에 만났어요. _____

(4)   기온이 많이 내려갔어요.   _____

(5)   구름이 많이 끼었어요.   _____

3. Using ~어/아질 거예요, make a prediction about the change of state resulting from the given situation.

(1)   날씨가 더웠는데 비가 왔어요.

       시원해질 거예요.

(2)   겨울이 되었어요.

       _____

(3)   이번 학기에 외국어를 세 과목 들어요.

       _____

(4)   학교가 너무 멀어서 이번 주말에 기숙사로 이사해요.

       _____

(5)   여름이라서 사람들이 여행을 많이 해요.

       _____

G1.2 | Sentence ending ~잖아요 'You know, . . .' (assuming agreement)

Examples

(1) A: 오늘 야외에서 수업해요?
B: 네, 날씨가 좋**잖아요**.

(2) A: 토요일에 콘서트에 같이 갈래요?
B: 저는 못 가요. 주말에 일하**잖아요**.

(3) A: 방 공기가 차네요.
B: 에어컨을 틀었**잖아요**.

(4) A: 제니 씨가 이번 시험에 A+를 받았어요.
B: 그동안 열심히 공부했**잖아요**.

Notes

1. This construction is used when the speaker assumes that the listener will agree with him/her. It is used when the speaker wants to reconfirm facts already known.

2. Although this form originated from a negative question (~지 않아요?), the intonation is not that of a question.

Exercises

1. Look at the pictures and provide an appropriate response.

(1)

A: 날씨가 추워졌어요.

B: 비가 오잖아요.

(2)

A: 학생들이 밖에 나가고
싶어해요.

B: _____

(3)   A: 스티브 씨가 이번 주에
                                     학교에 안 오네요.

                               B: _____

(4)   A: 리사가 한국어를 잘 하네요.

                               B: _____

(5)   A: 피곤한데 집에 택시 타고
                                     갈까요?

                               B: _____

2. Give an appropriate response to the following statements.

(1)   (A and B have been working hard since early in the
       morning.)
       A: 배가 고프네요.

       B: <u>벌써 오후 2시잖아요. 스파게티 먹으러 가요.</u>

(2)   (A and B have been studying in the library for three hours.)
       A: 굉장히 피곤하네요.

       B: _____

(3)   (A calls his girlfriend long-distance every day.)
       A: 이번 달에 전화비가 많이 나왔어요.

       B: _____

(4)   (우진 and five of his friends went to a restaurant.)
       A: 음식값이 굉장히 많이 나왔네요.

       B: _____

(5)   (A and B know that Steve has been playing tennis since
       childhood.)
       A: 스티브 씨는 테니스를 참 잘 치네요.

       B: _____

Conversation 2 　날씨가 추워졌네요.

(학교 앞에서 민지와 스티브가 만났습니다.)

민지: 스티브 씨, 안녕하세요? 오늘 참 춥지요?
따뜻하던[G1.3] 날씨가 어젯밤부터 갑자기
추워졌네요.

스티브: 비가 온 다음에는[G1.4] 날씨가 추워지잖아요.

민지: 아파트는 따뜻해요?

스티브: 보통은 따뜻한데, 어젯밤에는 난방이
안 돼서 굉장히 추웠어요.

민지: 어머, 그랬어요? 고생하셨겠네요.
이번 주말엔 날씨가 따뜻했으면 좋겠어요.[G1.5]

스티브: 참, 이번 주말에 잠실 운동장에서
야구 시합이 있는데,
같이 안 갈래요?

민지: 아, 그럴까요?

스티브: 두꺼운 옷을
입고 오세요.
지난 번에
야구장에
갔을 때는
바람이 불어서 추워서 혼났어요.

COMPREHENSION QUESTIONS

1. 그동안 날씨가 어땠습니까?
2. 언제부터 갑자기 추워졌습니까?
3. 스티브는 왜 어젯밤에 춥게 잤습니까?
4. 어디에서 야구 시합을 합니까?
5. 야구장에 갈 때 왜 두꺼운 옷을 입고 가야 합니까?

NEW WORDS

NOUN		VERB	
고생(하다)	hardship	계속되다	to continue
난방	heating	불다	to blow
데이트(하다)	a date	알리다	to inform
도	degree	없어지다	to disappear
라디오	radio	추워지다	to get colder
물건	merchandise	혼나다	to have a hard time
바람	wind	흐려지다	to get cloudy
섭씨	Celsius	**ADJECTIVE**	
시합	game, match	더럽다	to be dirty
야구(하다)	baseball	두껍다	to be thick
야구장	baseball stadium	**ADVERB**	
운동장	schoolyard, field	갑자기	suddenly
일기예보	weather forecast	꼭	surely, certainly
잠실	Jamsil	대체로	generally, mostly
프로	program	먼저	first, beforehand
현재	the present	**SUFFIX**	
		~(으)ㄴ 다음에	after ~
		~(으)면 좋겠다	I wish
		~던	used to

NEW EXPRESSIONS

1. 난방이 안 되다 means 'the heating system does not work'. 되다 'to become' has one of the most common idiomatic verbs, as shown in the usages below.

봄이 되었다.   Spring has come.
오 년이 되었다.   It has been five years.

키가 육 피트가 됩니다.	He is six feet tall. (amount to)
밥이 잘 안 되었다.	The rice did not turn out very well. (result)
준비가 다 되었다.	It is ready.
비즈니스가 잘 됩니다.	Business is good.
인터넷이 안 돼요.	The Internet does not work.

2. 굉장히 means 'very, extremely, enormously'. Similar adverbs are 무척, 아주, 몹시, 참 and 되게 (colloquial).

3. 혼나다 means 'to get frightened out of one's wits, have a bitter experience, get scolded (by someone)'. In the text, the meaning is 'to have a hard time' or 'to suffer a lot'. Literally 혼 means 'the spirit' or 'the soul' and 나다 is 'to go out'.

GRAMMAR

G1.3　Noun-modifying form ~던 (retrospective)

Examples

(1)　A:　춥**던** 날씨가 갑자기 따뜻해졌어요.
　　　　The weather, which had been cold, became cold suddenly.
　　B:　네. 일기예보를 봤는데 현재 기온이 섭씨 20도나 돼요.
　　　　Yes. The temperature has reached 20 degrees Celsius, according to the weather forecast.

(2)　A:　재미있**던** 코미디 프로가 언제부터 없어졌어요?
　　B:　지난 봄부터 없어졌어요.

(3)　크**던** 옷이 작아졌어요.

(4)　A:　한국에 가면 뭐 하고 싶어요?
　　B:　어렸을 때 살**던** 집에 가 보고 싶어요.

(5)　내가 전에 데이트하**던** 남자가 다른 여자와 사귀어요.

Notes

1. With the noun-modifying suffix ~던, the speaker describes an actual past situation (event or state) as if he/she were observing or perceiving it at the moment.

2. Often the meaning implies that the past situation does not exist any longer. When attached to an adjective stem, ~던 implies a change from the past state, as in (1) – (3).

3. When it is attached to a verb stem, on the other hand, it may mean a habitual action that did not continue. In this case, it renders the meaning of 'used to', as in (4) and (5).

Adjectives

~던	~(으)ㄴ	~(으)ㄹ
좋던	좋은	좋을
따뜻하던	따뜻한	따뜻할

(i)   좋던 날씨가 흐려졌어요.
       The weather, which had been good, became cloudy.
(ii)   좋은 사람을 만났어요.
       I met a nice person.
(iii) 내일 날씨가 좋을 거예요.
       Tomorrow the weather will be nice.

Verbs

~던	~(으)ㄴ	~는	~(으)ㄹ
읽던 책	읽은 책	읽는 책	읽을 책
다니던 학교	다닌 학교	다니는 학교	다닐 학교

(i)   어제 읽던 책이 없어졌어요.
       The book I was reading yesterday disappeared.
(ii)   이게 어제 읽은 책이에요?
       Is this the book you read yesterday?
(iii) 지금 읽는 책 재미있어요?
       Is the book you are reading now fun?

(iv)　내일 읽을 책이 많아요?

　　　Do you have a lot of books to read tomorrow?

Exercises

1. Complete the following sentences.

(1)　<u>하얗던</u> 눈이 더러워졌습니다.

(2)　＿＿＿＿＿＿ 옷이 깨끗해졌습니다.

(3)　＿＿＿＿＿＿ 날씨가 더워졌습니다.

(4)　＿＿＿＿＿＿ 동생이 키가 커졌습니다.

(5)　＿＿＿＿＿＿ 교통이 편리해졌습니다.

(6)　＿＿＿＿＿＿ 아버지가 시간이 많아지셨습니다.

2. Translate the following sentences.

(1)　This is the restaurant I used to go to often last year.

　　　＿＿＿＿＿＿＿＿＿＿＿＿＿＿＿＿＿＿＿＿

(2)　The TV program I used to watch nine years ago was *Dooly*.

　　　＿＿＿＿＿＿＿＿＿＿＿＿＿＿＿＿＿＿＿＿

(3)　Boston is a place where I used to live eleven years ago.

　　　＿＿＿＿＿＿＿＿＿＿＿＿＿＿＿＿＿＿＿＿

G1.4　V.S.~(으)ㄴ 다음에/후에 'after doing (something)'

Examples

(1)　A:　9시 수업이 끝**난 다음에** 뭐 해요?

　　　B:　한국어 연습하러 컴퓨터 랩에 가요.

(2)　A:　날씨가 많이 추워졌네요.

　　　B:　비가 **온 다음에**는 기온이 내려가잖아요.

(3)   A: 대학 졸업**한 후에** 뭐 하실 거예요?
       B: 대학원에 가고 싶어요.

(4)   A: 오늘 저녁은 밖에 나가서 먹을까요?
       B: 네, 옷을 갈아입**은 다음에** 휴게실에서 만나요.

(5)   날씨를 알려 드리겠습니다.
       장마가 끝**난 후에**는 대체로 맑은 날씨가 계속되겠습니다.

Notes

1. When one event has occurred before another one starts, ~(으)ㄴ 다음에/
후에 is used. This construction is similar to ~고 나서, as in 아홉 시 수업이
끝나고 나서 뭐 해요?

2. 부터 'from' can be added to this construction to mean "from/since the
time when . . ." as in 비가 온 다음부터 추워졌어요 and 아침을 먹은 후부터
숙제를 했어요.

Exercises

1. Complete the sentences using ~(으)ㄴ 다음에/후에.

(1)   먼저 영화를 봐요.
       먼저 영화를 본 다음에 슈퍼마켓에 가요.
(2)   한국어를 배워요.

       _____

(3)   식당에서 주문해요.

       _____

(4)   컴퓨터로 메일을 보내요.

       _____

(5)   돈을 많이 벌어요.

       _____

(6)   내년에 졸업해요.

       _____

2. Look at the following pictures and describe the events in sequence using ~(으)ㄴ 다음에/후에.

(1)　a.　　　　　b.

　　c.　　　　　d.

(2)　a.　　　　　b.

　　c.　　　　　d.

G1.5 Expressing speaker's wish: ~(으)면 좋겠다

Examples

(1)　A:　요즘 많이 춥지요?
　　B:　네, 빨리 봄이 **오면 좋겠어요.**

(2)   A: 돈이 많**으면 좋겠어요**.
       B: 돈이 많으면 뭐 하고 싶은데요?
       A: 집을 꼭 사고 싶어요.

(3)   A: 밤에 영화 볼래요?
       B: 피곤해서 잤**으면 좋겠어요**.

(4)   A: 날씨가 너무 덥네요.
       B: 바람 좀 불었**으면 좋겠지요**?

Notes

This construction ~(으)면 좋겠어요 means "It'd be nice if . . . were the case" but can be translated as "I wish . . ." The meaning of strong wish is expressed when the past-tense marker is used with ~(으)면, as in 친구가 빨리 왔으면 좋겠어요.

Exercises

1. Answer the following questions, using ~(으)면 좋겠어요.

(1)   내일 뭐 하고 싶어요? (등산가다)
       <u>등산 갔으면 좋겠어요</u>.

(2)   어젯밤에 잘 못 잤어요? (지금 쉬다)

       _____

(3)   시장에 가야 해요? (좋은 물건을 싸게 사다)

       _____

(4)   유럽에 가 봤어요? (가 보다)

       _____

(5)   친구하고 영화 보러 가요? (재미있다)

       _____

(6)   한국에서 뭘 할 거예요? (한국어를 공부하다)

       _____

2. What would you wish in the following situations? Answer in Korean.

    (1)   The soup is too salty.

    (2)   You just found out that there is an exam tomorrow.

    (3)   Your credit card has reached its limit.

    (4)   You need to call home, but you cannot find a phone nearby.

Narration 일기예보

안녕하십니까? 오늘 날씨를 알려 드리겠습니다.
아침에는 따뜻하고 맑겠지만 낮부터는 흐려져서 구름이
많이 끼겠고 저녁 때는 비가 오기 시작하겠습니다.
오늘 아침 기온은 섭씨 6도, 낮 기온은 13도가 되겠습니다.
내일 아침 기온은 오늘보다 낮아지고 찬 바람이
불겠습니다. 낮부터 맑아져서 서울은 주말까지 대체로
좋은 날씨가 계속되겠습니다. 서울의 현재 기온은 9
도입니다. 감기 조심하십시오.

COMPREHENSION QUESTIONS

1. 오늘 아침 날씨는 어떻습니까?
2. 언제부터 비가 오기 시작합니까?
3. 내일 아침에는 오늘 아침보다 더 따뜻해집니까?
4. 서울의 주말 날씨는 어떻습니까?

NEW EXPRESSIONS

1. Some of the common terms used in 일기예보 'weather forecast' are:

맑다	to be clear
흐리다	to be cloudy
구름이 끼다	to get cloudy
비가 오다	to rain
눈이 오다	to snow
바람이 불다	the wind blows

2. Change of temperature (기온) is expressed by 낮아지다 and 높아지다. A degree (도) of temperature is indicated exclusively by 섭씨 'Celsius' and not by 화씨 'Fahrenheit' in Korea.

기온이 낮아진다.	The temperature goes down.
기온이 높아진다.	The temperature goes up.

$$C = (F-32) \times 5/9 \qquad F = C \times 9/5 + 32$$

섭씨 C	-10°	0°	10°	20°	30°	36.5°	100°
화씨 F	14°	32°	50°	68°	83°	97.7°	212°

3. 알리다 'to inform, announce' is often used with the benefactive auxiliary verb 드리다 or 주다 'to do for', as in:

선생님께 이 뉴스를 알려 드려야 해요.	We have to inform the teacher of this news (for him/her).
내일까지 알려 주세요.	Inform me by tomorrow (for me).

4. 계속하다 'to continue something' is a transitive verb (a verb taking an object) while 계속되다 'something continues' is an intransitive verb (a verb without an object).

수업을 계속했습니다.   (The teacher) continued the class.
수업이 계속되었습니다.   The class continued.

CULTURE

음력과 양력: The use of the lunar and solar (Gregorian) calendars

한국에서는 양력과 음력을 다 씁니다. 옛날에는 음력만 썼지만 1896 년부터 양력도 같이 쓰기 시작했습니다. 음력은 달의 모양이 바뀌는 것을 보고 만든 달력입니다. 음력으로 한 달이 29일 또는 30일이 될 수도 있습니다. 옛날부터 음력은 농사와 어업에 아주 중요했습니다.

한국의 국경일들은 모두 양력을 씁니다. 그렇지만 아주 큰 명절들은 (설날, 추석) 음력을 쓰고 있습니다. 그리고 생일에 음력을 쓰는 사람들이 많습니다. 그래서 보통 한국의 달력에는 양력 날짜와 음력 날짜가 모두 있습니다.

국경일	national holidays	양력	solar calendar
날짜	date	어업	fishery
농사	farming	옛날	the old days
달	moon	음력	lunar calendar
달력	calendar	명절	traditional holidays
모양	shape		

USAGE

1. Describing weather

Examples

(1)　성희:　오늘 날씨 참 좋지요?
　　　마크:　네, 정말 좋은데요.
　　　　　　성희 씨는 어느 계절을 제일 좋아하세요?
　　　성희:　저는 가을이 제일 좋아요.
　　　　　　날씨도 시원해지고 공기도 깨끗하잖아요.
　　　　　　마크 씨는 어느 계절이 좋으세요?
　　　마크:　저는 스키도 탈 수 있고 방학도 길어서 겨울이 더
　　　　　　좋아요.

(2)　A:　오늘 날씨가 어때요?
　　　B:　공기가 맑고 시원해요.
　　　A:　어제 날씨는 어땠어요?
　　　B:　바람이 불고 추웠어요.
　　　A:　날씨가 좋으면 이번 주말에 뭐 하고 싶으세요?
　　　B:　바닷가에 수영하러 갔으면 좋겠어요.

Useful expressions

봄:　따뜻한 날씨
　　　꽃이 피는 날씨 (the weather when flowers bloom)
　　　맑은 날씨

여름:　더운 날씨
　　　　갑자기 비가 오는 날씨
　　　　무더운 날씨 (hot and humid weather)
　　　　장마 (the summer rainy season)

가을:　시원한 날씨
　　　　쌀쌀한 날씨 (chilly weather)
　　　　단풍이 들다 (to put on the tints of autumn foliage)

겨울: 눈이 오는 날씨
        얼음이 얼다 (ice forms)
        흐린 날씨
        공기가 건조하다 (dry air)

[Exercise 1] Ask your partner the following questions and report the result to the class.

(1)   어느 계절을 제일 좋아하세요? 왜요?

(2)   흐리고 비가 오는 날에는 보통 뭐 하는 걸 좋아하세요?

(3)   이번 주말에 날씨가 좋으면 뭐 하고 싶으세요?

(4)   날씨가 추운 날/비가 오는 날/눈이 오는 날/바람이 많이 부는 날 무슨 옷을 입으세요?

[Exercise 2] Report the four seasons where you live and say what effect the weather has on you.

[Exercise 3] Read the following weather map of Korea and answer the questions.

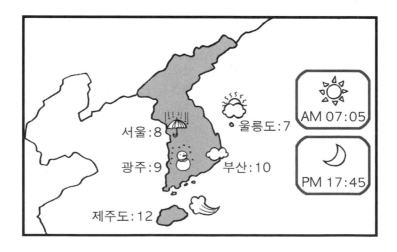

(1)   서울에 비가 올까요?

(2)   어느 곳이 제일 시원할까요?

(3)   서울과 부산은 어디가 더 덥습니까?

(4)   해가 지는 시간은 어떻게 됩니까? (해 지는 시간 sunset)

(5)   달이 뜨는 시간은 어떻게 됩니까? (달 뜨는 시간 moonrise)

(6)   지금은 겨울입니까? 봄입니까?

(7)   제주도의 날씨는 어떻습니까?

2. Indicating possibility and capability

Examples

(1)   A: 날씨가 좋으면 밖에서 무슨 운동을 할 수 있어요?

        B: 테니스도 칠 수 있고 골프도 칠 수 있어요.

        A: 날씨가 추울 때는 무슨 운동을 할 수 있어요?

        B: 스키도 탈 수 있고 농구(basketball)도 할 수 있어요.

(2)   A: 테니스 칠 줄 아세요?

        B: 네, 배웠는데 잘 못 쳐요.

(3)   A: 한국어를 컴퓨터로 칠 줄 아세요?

        B: 네, 할 수 있어요.

[Exercise 1] 무엇을 할 줄 아세요? Converse with your partner about three items in each given category about what you can do. When you have finished, change partners.

	1	2	3
노래			
외국어			
운동			
요리			

[Exercise 2] What can you do under the following weather conditions?

     (1)   비 오는 날:

     (2)   바람 부는 날:

     (3)   눈 오는 날:

     (4)   추운 날:

     (5)   더운 날:

3. Listening to weather forecasts

Examples

(1)   Narration

안녕하십니까? 오늘 날씨를 알려 드리겠습니다. 아침에는 따뜻하고
맑겠지만 낮부터는 흐려져서 구름이 많이 끼겠고 저녁때는 비가 오기
시작하겠습니다. 오늘 아침 기온은 섭씨 6도, 낮 기온은 13도가 되겠습니다.
내일은 낮부터 맑아져서 서울은 주말까지 좋은 날씨가 계속되겠습니다.
내일은 아침 기온은 오늘보다 낮아지고 찬바람이 불겠습니다. 감기
조심하십시오.

(2)   텔레비전 일기예보

내일 아침 서울 지방은 기온이 영하 5도까지 떨어지는 다소 추운 날씨가
되겠습니다. 하지만 낮부터 기온이 올라가면서 비교적 포근하겠습니다.
이번 달은 맑고 건조한 날씨가 계속되겠습니다.

(change of screen)
각 지방의 내일 날씨입니다. 중부 지방은 대체로 맑겠습니다. 강원, 영서

지방은 아침에 안개 끼는 곳이 있겠습니다. 남부와 제주도 지방은 오전에 흐리다가 오후부터 차차 맑아지겠습니다. 아침 최저 기온은 오늘보다 낮겠지만 낮 최고 기온은 오늘보다 높아져 포근하겠습니다.

Useful words

각 each, 기온 temperature, 영하 below the freezing point, 다소 more or less/to some degree, 비교적 relatively, 포근하다 to be warm, 건조한 dry, 화면 a (television) screen, 지방 region, 중부 지방 the central districts, 대체로 generally, 맑다 to be clear, 강원 Gangwon region, 영서 Youngseo region, 안개 끼다 to be foggy, 남부 southern, 차차 gradually, 최저 the lowest, 최고 the highest

[Exercise 1] Use the weather forecast (1) above and converse with another student as in the example.

Example:　　　Student 1:　　오늘 낮 날씨는 어때요?
　　　　　　　Student 2:　　흐리고 구름이 많이 낄 거예요.

[Exercise 2] Based on the weather forecast (2) above, answer the following questions.

    (1)　　　내일 아침 서울의 오전과 오후 날씨는 어떻습니까?

    (2)　　　이번 달의 날씨는 어떻습니까?

    (3)　　　내일 아침 안개가 끼는 곳은 어느 지방입니까?

    (4)　　　내일 남부 지방과 제주도의 오전 날씨는 어떻습니까?

[Exercise 3] Listen to the weather forecast announcement made by your teacher and answer questions.

[Exercise 4] Find a weather forecast for your town in the newspaper and report it to the class in Korean.

Lesson 1. Weather and Seasons

CONVERSATION 1: Which season do you like most?

(Minji and Mark are talking in front of the library.)

Minji: The weather has become a lot cooler, hasn't it?

Mark: Yes, it has become very cool. The summer has finished and it has already become autumn. This summer was boring because the rainy season lasted unusually long.

Minji: Mark, which season do you like most?

Mark: I like spring the most. You know, because the weather is warm and the flowers bloom a lot. How about you, Minji?

Minji: I like winter better because I can ski and, also, the school vacation is long.

Mark: Do you? Then, you must long for the winter, Minji.

Minji: Yes, but I also like autumn because I can see the autumn foliage. By the way, Mark, I will go to Seorak Mount in October to see the autumn foliage. Do you want to go with me?

Mark: To see the autumn foliage? I wanted to see it even before you mentioned it, so it works out well.

CONVERSATION 2: The weather has become cold.

(Minji and Steve meet in front of the school.)

Minji: Steve, how are you? Today it is very cold, isn't it? The weather was warm but has suddenly become colder since last night.

Steve: You know, the weather becomes colder after rain.

Minji: Is your apartment warm?

Steve: It is usually warm, but last night the heating didn't work, so it was very cold.

Minji: Oh, was it? You must have had a hard time. It will be nice if it is warm this weekend.

Steve: By the way, there is a baseball game at Jamsil Stadium this weekend. Will you go with me?

Minji: Oh, should I?

Steve: Wear thick clothes. The last time I went to the baseball stadium, I had a hard time because the wind made it cold.

NARRATION: Today's weather

How are you? Let me announce today's weather. In the morning, it will be warm and clear. However, at noon it will become overcast, so there will be many clouds in the sky. In the evening it will begin to rain. This morning's temperature is 6 degrees Celsius. The daytime temperature will rise to 13 degrees Celsius. Tomorrow morning's temperature will be lower than today's, and there will be a cold wind blowing. The sky will become clearer throughout the day, and Seoul will have mostly good weather until the weekend. The current temperature in Seoul is 9 degrees. Watch out for the cold.

CULTURE: Lunar and solar calendars

People use both the lunar and solar (Gregorian) calendars in Korea. A long time ago, they used only the lunar calendar, but since 1896 they have used the solar (Gregorian) calendar as well. The lunar calendar follows the phases of the moon. One month can be either twenty-nine days or thirty days by the lunar calendar. It was very important in agriculture and fishing long ago.

All the Korean national holidays follow the solar calendar. However, some traditional holidays (New Year's Day, Thanksgiving Day) follow the lunar calendar. And many people follow the lunar calendar for their birthdays. Therefore, Korean calendars usually have both solar and lunar dates.

2과 옷과 유행 [Clothing and Fashion]

Conversation 1 | 백화점에서 옷을 사려고 해요.

(수빈이 민지에게 전화를 합니다.)

수빈: 민지 씨, 지금 백화점에서 세일하는데
같이 안 갈래요?

민지: 마침 잘 됐네요. 저도 백화점에 가려고
지금 준비하고 있었는데. 저는 정장 한 벌을
사려고 하는데[G2.1] 수빈 씨는 뭐 사실 거예요?

수빈: 저는 원피스하고 구두를 하나 사려고요.
요즘 입을 옷이 없어서요.

민지: 저도 그래요. 한국은 옷 입는 스타일이
캐나다하고 달라서 옷 입기가 어렵네요.[G2.2]

수빈: 민지 씨는 어떤 정장이 필요하세요?

민지: 인터뷰가 있어서 단정한 치마 정장을
하나 사야 돼요.

COMPREHENSION QUESTIONS

1. 수빈이는 백화점에서 무엇을 사려고 합니까?
2. 왜 한국에서는 옷 입기가 어렵습니까?
3. 민지는 어떤 정장을 사려고 합니까?

NEW WORDS

NOUN		VERB	
구두	dress shoes	닫다	to close
굽	heel	(나이가) 들다	to gain age
단어	vocabulary	(마음에) 들다	to be to one's liking
마음	mind, heart	떠나다	to leave
반값	half price	(돈을) 벌다	to earn (money)
반바지	shorts	외우다	to memorize
블라우스	blouse	**ADJECTIVE**	
샌들	sandals	높다	to be high
스타일	style	단정하다	to be neat
원피스	(one-piece) dress	얇다	to be thin
유행(하다)	fashion, trend	필요하다	to be necessary
자켓	jacket	**ADVERB**	
정가	regular price	마침	just, just in time
정장	suit, formal dress	아식노	yet, still
치마	skirt	함께	together, along with
카메라	camera	**SUFFIX**	
현금	cash	~(으)려고 하다	intend to
COUNTER		~기가 쉽다/	it is easy/
벌	a pair of (counter)	어렵다	difficult to . . .

NEW EXPRESSIONS

1. 세일, 바겐 세일 'a bargain sale'

   백화점에서 세일을 해요.   There is a sale in the department store.

   이 옷은 세일이에요.   These clothes are on sale.

2. 마침 'coincidentally, as it just happens'

   친구한테 전화를 하려고 했는데 마침 친구한테서 전화가 왔어요.

   마침 돈이 있어서 필요한 책을 살 수 있었어요.

A: 저 지금 우체국에 가는데 필요한 거 있으면 말씀하세요.

B: 마침 잘 됐네요. 우표 좀 사다 주세요.

3. 바지 한 벌 'one pair of pants', 옷 한 벌 'one suit', 투피스 세 벌 'three women's suits', 양복 두 벌 'two men's suits', 청바지 네 벌 'four pairs of blue jeans'.

4. 필요하다 'to need, be necessary' is an adjective, unlike the English verb "need". Thus, it is used with the particle 이/가, as in 책이 필요합니다, not 책을 필요합니다.

GRAMMAR

G2.1   V.S.~(으)려고 'intending to'; V.S.~(으)려고 하다 'intend to'

Examples

[~(으)려고]

(1)   A: 어디 가세요?

      B: 얇은 자켓하고 반바지 사**려고** 백화점에 가요.

(2)   A: 뭐 하**려고** 은행에서 현금을 찾았어요?

      B: 친구와 함께 여행 가고 싶어서요.

(3)   A: 왜 경제학을 공부해요?

      B: 돈을 많이 벌**려고**요.

[~(으)려고 하다]

(4)   A: 오늘 카메라 안 사세요?

      B: 크리스마스 세일할 때 반값에 사**려고요**.

      A: 정가가 얼마인데요?

      B: 300,000원이요.

(5)   A: 비가 오**려고 하네요**.

      B: 어제부터 날씨가 흐렸지요?

(6)   A: 세일 때 뭐 좀 샀어요?

       B: 청바지 하나 사**려고** 했는데 바빠서 못 갔어요.

(7)   A: 오늘도 늦게 잘 거예요?

       B: 오늘은 피곤해서 일찍 자**려고요**.

Notes

1. ~(으)**려고** is mainly used to express the speaker's intention or plan. It also has the meaning of 'being about to', in addition to 'in an effort to' and 'intending to'.

건강해지려고 매일 운동합니다. (in an effort to)
신문을 읽으려고 샀습니다. (intending to)
성희는 일찍 자려고 합니다. (plan)
버스가 떠나려고 합니다. (be about to)

2. Unlike ~(으)러, which is followed only by a verb of going and coming, there is no such constraint with ~(으)려고.

옷을 한 벌 사러 백화점에 갔어요.
옷을 한 벌 사려고 백화점에 갔어요.
공부를 하려고 책을 한 권 샀어요.
공부를 하러 책을 한 권 샀어요. (X)

3. In colloquial speech, ~(으)ㄹ라(구) 그래요 or ~(으)ㄹ라구 해요 is often used instead of ~(으)려고 해요. Also, the verb 하다 can be omitted from the suffix ~(으)려고 (해)요 as in (7).

Exercises

1. Using ~(으)려고, answer the following questions.

(1)   A: 웬일이세요?

       B: 사전 좀 빌리려고 전화했어요.

(2)   A: 왜 한국말을 공부해요?

       B: _____

(3)   A: 왜 은행에서 돈을 많이 찾았어요(withdraw money)?

B: _____

(4)   A: 왜 이 식당에 자주 와요?

B: _____

(5)   A: 왜 한국에 왔어요?

B: _____

2. Using ~(으)려고 하다, ask your partner what he/she plans to do in the following situations.

(1)   A: 여름 방학에 뭐 하려고 하세요?

B: 많이 쉬고 싶어요. 그리고 여행도 하려고 해요.

(2)   A: 이번 주말에 _____

B: _____

(3)   A: 오늘밤 자기 전에 _____

B: _____

(4)   A: 다음 주 여행 떠나기 전에 _____

B: _____

| G2.2 | V.S.~기(가) 쉽다/어렵다 'it is easy/difficult to . . .' |

Examples

(1)   A: 한국에서 옷 입기가 어때요?
       B: 미국하고 스타일이 달라서 옷 입**기가 참 어려워요**.

(2)   A: 아직도 블라우스 못 샀어요?
       B: 네, 마음에 드는 걸 찾**기가 어렵네요**.

(3)   A: 어디가 불편하세요?
       B: 샌들 굽이 높아서 걷**기가 힘들어요**.

Notes

1. ~기(가) 쉽다/어렵다 is used to comment on how easy or difficult it is to do a certain action.

2. Other adjectives may be used to comment on other aspects of the action:

~기(가) 힘들다	it is difficult to . . .
~기(가) 좋다	it is easy/convenient to use for . . .
~기(가) 편하다/불편하다	it is convenient/inconvenient to . . .
~기(가) 싫다	I don't want to . . .

나이가 들면 단어 외우는 것이 힘들어요.
서울에서는 지하철 타기가 편리해요.

3. Compare ~기(가) 좋다 with ~는 것이/게 좋다. ~는 것이/게 좋다 means 'doing . . . is good for you' or 'you'd better do . . .,' while 하기 좋다 means 'it is convenient . . .'

어렸을 때 외국어 공부를 열심히 하는 게 좋아요.

Exercises

1. Give a few examples that belong to each category.

(1)	쓰기 쉬운 컴퓨터:	_____
(2)	읽기 어려운 책:	_____
(3)	먹기 싫은 음식:	_____
(4)	운전하기 좋은 차:	_____
(5)	듣기 좋은 음악:	_____
(6)	신기 편한 신발:	_____
(7)	하기 쉬운 운동:	_____
(8)	살기 불편한 곳:	_____

2. Complete the following sentences using ~기 어렵다/힘들다/쉽다/
편하다/불편하다/좋다/싫다.

(1)   일요일 밤에 파티를 자주 해요. 그래서 <u>월요일에는 일찍</u>
       <u>일어나기가 힘들어요</u>.

(2)   밖이 시끄러워요. 그래서 _____

(3)   책값이 비싸요. 그래서 _____

(4)   주말에는 길이 많이 막혀요. 그래서 _____

       _____

(5)   늦은 밤에는 식당을 다 닫아요. 그래서 _____

       _____

(6)   새로 산 구두가 너무 작아요. 그래서 _____

       _____

Conversation 2 | 요즘 짧은 치마가 유행이에요.

(수빈이와 민지는 옷을 사러 백화점에 갔습니다)

점원: 어서 오세요. 어떤 옷을 찾으세요?

수빈: 구경 좀 할게요.

점원: 네, 천천히 골라 보세요.

수빈: 저기, 요즘 어떤 치마가 유행이에요?

점원: 요즘 짧은 치마가 유행인데 이거 어떠세요?

수빈: 초록색 말고[G2.3] 남색은 없어요?

점원: 요즘은 어두운 색보다 밝은 색이 인기가
         많아요. 노란색이나 하늘색은 어떠세요?

수빈: 그러면 둘 다 입어 봐도 돼요?[G2.4]

점원: 네, 그럼요.

수빈: 민지 씨, 저한테 어떤 색이 어울려요?

민지: 수빈 씨한테는 하늘색이 더 잘 어울리는 것
         같아요.[G2.5]

수빈: 그래요? (점원에게) 그럼 하늘색으로 주세요.

COMPREHENSION QUESTIONS

1. 수빈이는 무슨 옷을 사고 싶어합니까?
2. 수빈이는 무슨 옷을 입어 봤습니까?
3. 요즘 어떤 옷이 유행입니까?
4. 요즘 어떤 색이 인기가 많습니까?
5. 수빈이한테는 어떤 색이 잘 어울립니까?

NEW WORDS

NOUN		VERB	
가격	price	고르다	to choose, select
검정색	black	뛰다	to run
남색	navy blue, indigo	맞다	to fit
노란색	yellow	모자라다	to lack
담배	cigarette	바뀌다	to be changed
문제	problem	어울리다	to match, suit
빨간색	red	피우다	to smoke
(신용) 카드	credit card	**ADJECTIVE**	
와이셔츠	dress shirt	밝다	to be bright
인기	popularity	어둡다	to be dark
점퍼	jumper, jacket	**ADVERB**	
초록색	green	말고	not A but B
티셔츠	T-shirt	천천히	slowly
파란색	blue	**PARTICLE**	
하늘색	sky blue	(으)로	item selected
흰색	white		from among many
CONJUNCTIVE		**SUFFIX**	
그러면	then, in that case	~(으)ㄴ/는/(으)ㄹ 것 같다	it seems like
		~어/아도 되다	expresses permission

NEW EXPRESSIONS

1. While 유행 'fashion' is a noun, 유행하다 'to be in fashion, be in vogue' is a verb. So, the modifier form is 유행하는, as in 유행하는 옷, 유행하는 음악.

2. 유행하다 is an adjective meaning 'to be in fashion' while 유행이다 is a verb, though the meaning is similar.

> 긴 치마가 유행입니다.   Long skirts are in fashion.
> 긴 치마가 유행합니다.   Long skirts are in fashion.

The modifier forms are different because one is an adjective and the other is a verb as in

> 요즘 유행인 헤어스타일
> 요즘 유행하는 헤어스타일

3. 고르다 'to choose, select' is a 르-irregular verb, as in 골라요, 골라 주세요, 골랐어요, but 고르면, 고르세요.

4. 그럼 is a shortened form of the conjunctive 그러면/그렇다면 'then'. In discourse, 그럼요 is also used as 'I agree with you totally'.

5. 어울리다 'to look good (on), go well (with)' is used with the particle 한테 or 에게.

> 빨간색이 수미한테 잘 어울려요.
> Red looks good on Sumi.

G2.3   N1 말고 N2 'not N1 but N2'

Examples

(1)   A: 이 초록색 점퍼 어떠세요?
      B: 초록색 **말고** 빨간색으로 주세요.

(2)   A: 뉴스를 보고 싶은데요.
      B: 뉴스 **말고** 드라마를 보세요.

(3)   A: 육개장 드릴까요?
      B: 저는 육개장 **말고** 불고기를 시키려고 해요.

(4)   A: 이 원피스 어떠세요?

      B: 원피스 **말고** 바지 입어 볼게요.

Notes

1. When you choose one option over the other, 말고 is used after the first noun as shown above. Notice that it is normally used in command and proposal.

> 다음 학기에는 중국어 말고 한국어를 공부하세요.
> 티셔츠 말고 와이셔츠를 입는 게 어때요?

2. When an action is involved, a verb form is used, as in V.S.~지 말고.

> 내일이 시험이에요. 놀지 말고 공부하세요.
> 수업을 9시에 시작하지 말고 10시에 시작할까요?
> 도서관에서는 전화하지 말고 공부만 하세요.

Exercises

1. Give an alternative.

(1)   A: 지금 숙제할까요?

      B: <u>지금 말고 오후에 하면 어때요?</u>

           How about doing it in the afternoon instead of now?

(2)   A: 청소할까요?

      B: _____

(3)   A: 콘택트 렌즈(contact lens)를 낄까요?

      B: _____

(4)   A: 한국어를 전공할까요?

      B: _____

(5)   A: 저녁에 불고기를 먹을까요?

      B: _____

(6)   A: 흰색 점퍼를 살까요, 검정색 자켓을 살까요?

B: _____

2. Look at the pictures and suggest an item to your partner. Add a reason for your suggestion.

(1)   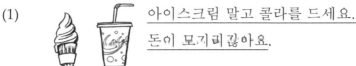   아이스크림 말고 콜라를 드세요.
돈이 모지리피깊아요.

(2)      _____

(3)      _____

(4)      _____

| G2.4 | Expressions of permission and prohibition: V.S.~어도/아도 되다; V.S.~(으)면 안 되다 |

Examples

(1)   A: 식당에서 담배 피**워도 돼요**?   Would it be okay to smoke at a restaurant?

B: 아니요, 피우**면 안 돼요**.   No, it is not.

(2)   A: 현금이 모자라는데
카드로 내**도 돼요**?   Can I pay with my card since I'm short of cash?

B: 네, 그럼요.   Yes, of course.

(3)   A: 단어 시험 볼 때 점심 먹**어도 될까요**?
       B: 아니요, 교실에서 먹**으면 안 돼요**.

(4)   A: 파티에 정장 입고 가야 돼요?
       B: 아니요, 정장 안 입**어도 돼요**/입지 **않아도 돼요**.

Notes

1. ~어도/아도 means 'even though, even if'. ~어도/아도 되다, literally meaning 'even though/if . . ., it is all right', is used to ask or grant permission. The negative form of ~어도/아도 되다 is 안 ~어도/아도 되다 or ~지 않아도 되다, as in (4).

괜찮다 'to be all right' or 좋다 'to be good' may be used instead of 되다 to be more specific with the meaning of permission.

2. ~(으)면 안 되다, literally meaning 'it is not all right, if . . .', is used to deny permission, prohibit a certain action, or give a warning.

Exercises

1. Provide an appropriate response in the given context.

(1)   [수업이 끝났습니다.]
       학생: 지금 집에 가도 돼요?
       선생님: 네, 가도 돼요. or 아니요, 지금 가면 안 돼요.

(2)   [학생이 교수님 연구실에 갔는데, 다른 학생이 벌써 있었습니다.]
       학생: 교수님, 밖에서 기다릴까요?
       교수님: 아니요, 괜찮아요. _____

(3)   학생: 선생님 오늘 숙제 내야 돼요?
       선생님: 아니요, _____
                    그렇지만 내일까지는 내야 돼요.

(4)   A: 수업 시간에 점심을 먹어도 돼요?
       B: _____

(5)   A: 이 전화 좀 써도 돼요?

       B: _____

2. Ask permission appropriately in the given context.

   (1)   [In a shoe store]

          A: <u>신발 좀 구경해도 돼요?</u>

          B: 그럼요. 천천히 구경하세요.

   (2)   [B is going to treat A in a restaurant. A wants to check
          if B has enough money.]

          A: _____?

          B: 먹고 싶은 거 시키세요.

                그렇지만 너무 비싼 건 시키지 마세요.

   (3)   [A needs to make an emergency call, so A goes into a store.]

          A: _____?

          B: 네, 쓰세요. 전화 여기 있어요.

   (4)   [A and B have an appointment at B's office, and A wants to
          come now.]

          A: _____?

          B: 네, 오세요.

   (5)   [Steve visits a professor.]

          스티브: _____?

          교수님: 잠깐만 기다리세요.

G2.5   ~(으)ㄴ/는/(으)ㄹ 것 같다 'it seems/looks like'

Examples

(1)   이 정장이 가격은 좀 비싸지만 저한테 잘 맞**는 것 같아요**.

(2)   A: 새로 산 구두 굽이 너무 높**은 것 같아요**.

       B: 그래요? 한번 신어 보세요.

(3)   A: 친구가 전화를 안 받아요.

       B: **여행 간 것 같아요**.

(4)   A: 내일부터 추워**질 것 같지요**?

       B: 네, 눈도 **올 것 같아요**.

(5)   A: 미나 씨가 노래를 정말 잘하지요?

       B: 네, 가수 **같아요**.

Notes

1. ~(으)ㄴ/는/(으)ㄹ 것 같다 is an expression of resemblance or approximation. Even when the speaker has no doubt, it is quite common to use this pattern, as an indirect, thus more polite, way of expression.

	Verb	Adjective
Past	어젯밤에 잘 잔 것 같아요.	시험이 쉬웠던 것 같아요.
Present	지금 잘 자는 것 같아요.	시험이 쉬운 것 같아요.
Future	오늘 밤에는 잘 잘 것 같아요.	시험이 쉬울 것 같아요.

2. Noun + 같다 'It looks like [noun]'.

       파란색 옷을 입은 분이 선생님 같아요.
       재미있는 영화 같은데요.
       저기에 옷이 많은 것 같은데, 들어가 볼까요?

3.   같아요 is often pronounced as [갈애요].
       . . . 것 같다 becomes [. . . 거 같다] in colloquial speech.

Exercises

1. Look at the following pictures and make observations.

(1)

밑이 추운 것 같아요.

(2)

_____

(3)

_____

(4)

_____

(5)

_____

(6)

_____

2. Respond to the following statements, using ~(으)ㄴ/는/(으)ㄹ 것 같다.

(1)   내일 날씨가 어떨까요?

   _____

(2)   시험 문제가 어려울까요?

   _____

(3)   빨간색이 저한테 잘 어울릴까요?

_____

(4)   밖에서 좀 뛰고 싶은데 날씨가 어때요?

_____

(5)   요즘 부모님 건강이 어떠세요?

_____

(6)   요즘 책 값이 어떤 것 같아요?

_____

(7)   어젯밤에 날씨가 어땠어요?

_____

(8)   요즘 서울 물가가 많이 올랐어요?

_____

Narration 백화점 쇼핑

오늘 수빈이는 친구 민지와 같이 옷을 사러 백화점에
갔습니다. 백화점 안은 쇼핑하러 온 사람들 때문에 아주
복잡했습니다. 수빈이는 요즘 유행하는 짧은 치마와
블라우스, 그리고 굽이 높은 샌들을 사고 민지는 운동할 때
입을 편한 바지와 티셔츠를 샀습니다. 한국은 유행이 자주
바뀌어서 옷 사기가 어렵습니다. 민지는 캐나다에 계시는
아버지께 드리려고 얇은 면 샤쓰도 하나 샀습니다. 세일을
해서 반값으로 싸게 살 수 있었습니다. 그런데 현금이
모자라서 카드로 냈습니다. 수빈이하고 민지는 마음에 꼭
드는 옷을 싸게 사서 기분이 아주 좋았습니다.

COMPREHENSION QUESTIONS

1. 백화점이 왜 복잡했습니까?
2. 수빈이가 산 물건들을 다 써 보세요.
3. 민지는 어떤 자켓을 골랐습니까?
4. 민지는 왜 카드로 냈습니까?
5. 수빈이는 왜 기분이 좋았습니까?

NEW EXPRESSIONS

(1) The verb 계시다 is the honorific version of the verb 있다 'to be, stay'. It could be used as a main verb as in (a) or an auxiliary verb as in (b).

> (a) 서울에 계시는 선생님께 편지를 썼어요.
> (b) 아버지는 책을 읽고 계세요.

(2) 마음에 꼭 들다 literally means '(Someone/something) exactly enters the heart'. It is synonymous with the verb 좋아하다, though it never takes an object. Note that this is a verb, not an adjective, so its modifying form takes ~는, as in 마음에 드는 옷.

> 이런 신발이 마음에 꼭 들어요.
> 이런 신발을 좋아해요.

CULTURE

한국의 의(衣)생활: The Korean life pertaining to clothes

한국은 미국과 옷 문화가 조금 다릅니다. 학교나 교회에 갈 때 그냥 슬리퍼를 신거나 짧은 치마나 반바지, 또는 소매가 없는 옷을 입는 것을 좋아하지 않습니다. 일을 하러 갈 때도 많은 사람들이 정장을 입습니다. 은행이나 우체국에서 일하는 사람들은 유니폼을 입기도 합니다. 중고등학교에서는 보통 교복을 입습니다.

어른을 만날 때도 깨끗하고 단정한 옷을 입으려고 합니다. 인터뷰할 때 남자는 넥타이를 매고 정장을 입어야 하고, 여자도 단정한 치마 정장이나 바지 정장을 입고 화려하지 않은 액세서리를 합니다. 설날이나 결혼식 등의 특별한 날에는 전통 옷인 한복을 입기도 합니다.

교복	school uniform	액세서리	accessory
단정하다	to be neat	어른	adult, (one's) elders
매다	to tie	유니폼	uniform
문화	culture	의생활	clothing habits
소매	sleeve	특별하다	to be special
슬리퍼	slipper	화려하다	to be fancy, colorful

USAGE

1. Requesting, granting, and denying permission

(Requesting and granting permission)

(1)　　점원:　어서 오세요. 어떤 옷을 찾으세요?
　　　　성희:　구경 좀 해도 돼요?
　　　　점원:　그럼요. 구경하세요.
　　　　성희:　이 치마 한 번 입어 봐도 될까요?
　　　　점원:　네, 입어 보세요.

(Asking permission)

(2)　　A:　저어, 머리가 많이 아픈데 집에 일찍 가도 됩니까?
　　　　B:　많이 아파요? 그럼 집에 가서 쉬세요.

(3)　　A:　숙제를 내일까지 내도 돼요?
　　　　B:　내일까지 내면 안 돼요. 오늘 내세요.

(4)　　A:　여기 있는 신문 좀 봐도 될까요?
　　　　B:　네, 보세요.

(Requesting and refusing)

(5)   A: 사전 있으면 좀 빌려 주실 수 있으세요?
        B: 사전이 없는데요.

(6)   A: 밖에 비가 많이 오는데, 우산 좀 빌려 주실래요?
        B: 저도 지금 나가야 되기 때문에 . . . 죄송합니다.

You can also ask permission by ~(으)면 안 돼요/안 될까요?

        A: 숙제를 아직 다 못 했는데 내일 내면 안 될까요?
        B: 네, 좋아요. 내일 주세요.

        A: 이 연습 문제가 어려운데 나중에 하면 안 돼요?
              (연습 문제 'an exercise')
        B: 안 돼요. 지금 하세요.

Here are different ways of making a request.

        밖에 비가 오는데 우산이 없어요.
        저어, 우산 있어요?
        저어, 죄송하지만 우산 좀 . . .
        혹시 우산 있으세요? (혹시 'by any chance')
        우산 좀 빌려 주실래요?
        우산 좀 빌려 주실 수 있으세요?
        죄송하지만 우산 좀 빌려 주세요.
        우산 좀 빌려도 될까요?
        우산 좀 빌릴 수 있을까요?
        우산 좀 빌렸으면 하는데요.

[Exercise 1] Use any of the above expressions to ask your teacher to do the following:

        (1)   lend you $20.00

        (2)   accept a late homework assignment

        (3)   speak Korean slowly

        (4)   not make tests too difficult

(5)   write Korean characters clearly

(6)   lend you a Korean textbook

[Exercise 2] Pair up and role-play for the following situations:

(1)   You just bought a black sweater at a department store. But you want to exchange it for a different color and style.

(2)   You are very hungry, but there is nothing to eat in the refrigerator except for the leftover Chinese food that your roommate brought from a Chinese restaurant last night. Ask your roommate for permission to eat it.

(3)   You are taking a two-hour final exam for an intermediate Korean class. You need to go to the restroom in the middle of the exam. Ask your teacher for permission. (화장실 'restroom')

(4)   You are at work and suddenly have a headache. You took a medicine, but it did not soothe. So you ask your boss for permission to leave early.

(5)   You are a Korean businessman at a large corporation. You have an important meeting in twenty minutes, and there are a lot of things you want your secretary to do. But there are a couple of things she is not willing to do. Play the role of boss and secretary.

[Exercise 3] Look at the following pictures and express prohibition.

(1)   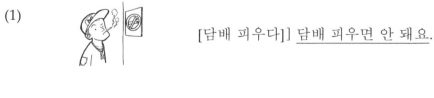 [담배 피우다]] 담배 피우면 안 돼요.

(2)    [앉다]_____

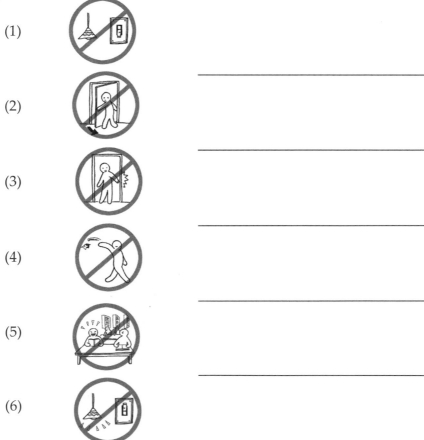

(3)   [들어가다]_____

(4)   [들어오다]_____

[Exercise 4] Express prohibition by ~지 마세요 or ~(으)면 안 돼요. (열다 'to open', 끄다 'to turn off', 켜다 'to turn on', 버리다 'to throw away')

(1)   _____

(2)   _____

(3)   _____

(4)   _____

(5)   _____

(6)   _____

2. Making plans

(1)   성희: 민지 씨, 백화점에서 지금 세일을 하는데,
          같이 안 가 볼래요?

      민지: 마침 잘 됐네요. 바지를 하나 사려고 했는데 . . .
          성희씨는 뭐 살 거예요?

      성희: 투피스 한 벌하고 구두를 하나 살까 해요.

(2)   A: 백화점에 언제 갈 거예요?
      B: 글쎄요, 내일 오후쯤 갈까 해요.

(3)   A: 콘서트에 안 갈래요? 티켓(ticket)이 두 장 있어요.
      B: 고마워요. 같이 가요.

(4)   A: 오늘 도서관에 갈 거예요?
      B: 네, 수업 끝나고 세 시쯤 가서 책 빌리려고 해요.

(5)   A: 오늘 저녁은 나가서 먹어요?
      B: 네, 기숙사 친구들하고 한국 식당에 가기로 했어요.
          같이 갈래요?

(6)   A: 선생님, 학기말 시험이 끝난 다음에 기숙사에서 파티 할
          건데 오실 수 있으세요?
      B: 네, 꼭 갈게요.

There are several ways of expressing one's intention.

할까 해요	I am thinking of doing . . .
하려고 해요	I plan to/intend to . . .
할 거예요	I will probably do . . .
할래요	I'll do . . .
할게요	I'd like to do . . . (volunteering)
하기로 했어요	I decided to do . . .

[Exercise 1] Role-play for the following situations.

(1)   You want to go shopping at a 'Back to school' sale to buy clothes, shoes, and stationery. Make a list of things to buy, then call a friend to go shopping together.

(2)   You and your friends are planning a surprise birthday party for someone. There are a lot of things to prepare: presents, cake, invitation cards, drinks, food, place, etc. Organize the party.

[Exercise 2] Make plans, using the "intention" constructions.

Example

지난 여름에는 여행을 할까 했는데, 시간도 없고 돈도 없어서 그냥 집에 있었어요. 이번 여름에는 꼭 뉴욕에 가려고 해요. 뉴욕에서 일하고 싶어서 뉴욕 월스트리트에 있는 회사(company)에 전화를 했어요. 다음 주에 인터뷰를 하기로 했어요.

(1)   summer plan
(2)   plan for next semester
(3)   plan for a friend's birthday party
(4)   plan for a weekend trip

3. Describing physical appearance

(1)   A: 비가 오는 날 어떤 옷을 입으세요?
       B: 청바지를 입고 긴 장화(boots)를 신어요.
       A: 바람이 많이 부는 날은 어떤 옷을 입으세요?
       B: 모자를 쓰고 스웨터를 입어요.

(2)   A: 결혼식(wedding)에 갈 때 어떤 옷을 입으세요?
       B: 보통 정장을 입어요.

(3) A: 이 옷이 어때요?

B: 잘 맞는데 소매(sleeve)가 길어요.

(4) A: 이 치마는 좀 긴 것 같아요.

B: 아니에요. 요즘은 긴 치마가 유행이에요.

(5) A: 남자 친구가 어떻게 생겼어요?

B: 키가 크고 잘 생겼어요. 영화 배우(actor) 같아요.

(6) A: 살이 빠진 것 같아요.

B: 요즘 운동해요.

Useful expressions

뚱뚱하다	to be fat
날씬하다	to be thin
말랐다	to be skinny
살이 찌다	to gain weight
살이 빠지다	to lose weight
다이어트하다	to be on a diet
키가 크다	to be tall
키가 작다	to be short
예쁘다	to be pretty
잘생기다	to be handsome
멋있다	to be stylish
못생기다	to be ugly
소매가 길다	the sleeves are long
옷이 맞다	the clothes fit
치마가 길다	the skirt is long
치마가 짧다	the skirt is short

[Exercise 1] Interview your classmates.

(1) 부모님보다 키가 크세요?

(2) 동생 있어요? 어떻게 생겼어요? 나이는 몇이에요?

(3) 어느 남자/여자 배우(actor)가 제일 잘생겼어요/예뻐요?

    (4)   어떤 사람과 결혼하고 싶어요?

    (5)   키가 작은 농구 선구가 있습니까?

    (6)   요즘 어떤 옷이 유행이에요?

    (7)   못생긴 영화 배우가 있어요? 누구예요?

    (8)   다이어트를 해 봤어요?

[Exercise 2] Converse with your classmates about their favorite outfits.

[Exercise 3] Choose several well-known people (e.g., celebrities, classmates, politicians, etc.). Let your classmates guess who you have in mind by giving them hints about their physical appearance.

[Exercise 4] Bring photos of your family or friends. Describe each person's physical appearance and outfits.

4. Shopping

(1)   (옷 가게에서)

    A: 어서 오세요. 뭘 찾으세요?

    B: 여름 티셔츠 좀 보려고요.

    A: 이 쪽에 좋은 게 많이 있습니다.
           무슨 색 찾으세요?

    B: 노란색 있어요?

    A: 노란색은 지금 없는데 다른 색으로 골라 보세요.

    B: 그럼 하늘색으로 주세요. 얼마예요?

    A: 정가(list price)는 이 만원인데 지금 세일이라서
           만 오천원입니다.

(2)   (구두 가게에서)

    A: 뭐 찾으세요?

    B: 네. 일할 때 신을 편한 구두를 찾고 있는데요.

    A: 무슨 사이즈(size) 신으세요?

    B: 240으로 주세요.

[Exercise 1] (Pair work) Engage in a dialogue between a store clerk and a customer to shop for the following items.

    (1)   긴 치마

    (2)   운동복

    (3)   목도리(muffler, scarf)와 장갑 (gloves)

    (4)   정장 구두 (dress shoes)

    (5)   와이셔츠와 넥타이 (dress shirt and necktie)

    (6)   겨울 코트 (coat)

    (7)   바지와 블라우스 (blouse)

[Exercise 2] Ask your classmate the following questions and report the result to the class.

    (1)   날씨가 추워지면 어떤 옷을 입으세요?

    (2)   더운 여름에는 보통 어떤 옷을 입으세요?

    (3)   봄 여름 가을 겨울 정장이 몇 벌이나 있어요?

    (4)   신발이 모두 몇 켤레 있어요?

    (5)   청바지가 모두 몇 벌 있어요?

    (6)   신발 사이즈 뭐 신으세요?

    (7)   옷을 얼마나 자주 사세요?

    (8)   옷을 보통 어디에서 사세요?

    (9)   갖고 있는 옷 중에서 비싼 옷이 어떤 옷이고 얼마예요?

    (10)   갖고 있는 옷 중에서 가장 자주 입는 옷은 뭐예요?

Lesson 2. Clothing and Fashion

CONVERSATION 1: I am going to buy clothes at the department store.

(Soobin makes a call to Minji.)

Soobin:	Minji, there is a sale at the department store. Do you want to go together?
Minji:	Just in time; this worked out well. I was just preparing to go to the department store as well now. I am going to buy a suit. What are you going to buy?
Soobin:	I am going to buy a dress and a pair of dress shoes. I don't have clothes to wear these days.
Minji:	Neither do I. It is hard to choose clothes because Korea has a different style from Canada.
Soobin:	What kind of suit do you need, Minji?
Minji:	I have to buy a decent skirt suit because I have an interview.

CONVERSATION 2: Miniskirts are trendy these days.

(Soobin and Minji are at the department store to buy clothes.)

Sales assistant:	Welcome. What kind of clothes are you looking for?
Soobin:	Let me look around.
SA:	OK, take your time to choose.
Soobin:	Well what kinds of skirts are trendy these days?
SA:	Miniskirts are trendy these days. How do you like this?
Soobin:	Do you have it in navy as well as in green?
SA:	Nowadays, bright colors are more popular than dark colors. How do you like the yellow or sky blue colors?
Soobin:	May I try both?
SA:	Yes, of course.
Soobin:	Minji, which color looks good on me?
Minji:	That sky blue color suits you better, Soobin.
Soobin:	Is that so? (To the sales assistant) Then, please give me the sky blue one.

NARRATION: Shopping at the department store

Today, Soobin went to the department store to buy clothes with her friend Minji. It was very crowded with people who came to shop at the department store. Soobin bought a miniskirt, which is trendy these days, a blouse, and high-heeled sandals; Minji bought a comfortable pair of pants to wear when she exercises, and T-shirts. It is hard to buy clothes because clothing trends change quickly in Korea. Minji bought a thin cotton jacket to give to her father, who is in Canada. The sale allowed her to buy it at half price. However, since she didn't have enough cash, she paid through her card. Soobin and Minji felt very good because they bought clothes that they liked at a cheap price.

CULTURE: The Korean life pertaining to clothes

Korea has a little different clothing culture from America. People don't like wearing slippers, miniskirts, short pants, or sleeveless clothes when going to school or church. Many people wear formal suits going to work. People who work at the banks or post offices tend to wear uniforms. Middle school and high school students usually wear school uniforms.

People try to wear clean and neat clothes when meeting elders. Men should wear a formal suit with a necktie, and women should wear a neat skirt suit or pant suit without fancy accessories for an interview. People sometimes wear the traditional Korean costume, *hanbok*, on special days such as New Year's Day or a wedding ceremony.

3과 여행 [Travel]

| Conversation 1 | 한국에 가게 됐어요. |

(소피아는 뉴욕대학 캠퍼스에서 마이클을 만났습니다.)

마이클: 안녕하세요, 소피아 씨. 어디 가세요?

소피아: 어, 마이클 씨, 전화하려고 했는데
　　　　마침 잘 만났네요.

마이클: 왜요?

소피아: 사실은 저 이번 여름에 한국에 가게 됐어요.^{G3.1}

마이클: 그래요? 잘 됐네요. 참, 스티브도 서울에
　　　　있는데 만나게 되면 스티브한테 제 안부 좀
　　　　전해 주세요.

소피아: 네, 그럴게요.

마이클: 비행기 표는
　　　　사셨어요?

소피아: 네, 벌써
　　　　예약했어요.

마이클: 한국까지
　　　　왕복에 얼마예요?

소피아: 1,600불이에요.

마이클: 비자는 필요 없어요?

소피아: 네, 여권만 있으면 돼요.^{G3.2}

COMPREHENSION QUESTIONS

1. 소피아는 이번 여름에 어디에 갑니까?
2. 스티브는 지금 어디 있습니까?
3. 소피아는 비자를 받았습니까?

NEW WORDS

NOUN		VERB	
가운데	center, the middle	다치다	to hurt
국내선	domestic flight	맞다	to be correct
국제선	international flight	싸다	to pack, wrap
농구	basketball	알아듣다	to understand,
무료	free		recognize
비자	visa	이해하다	to understand
사실	fact, truth	전하다	to tell, convey
손	hand	**ADJECTIVE**	
안부	regards	가볍다	to be light
여권	passport	무겁다	to be heavy
여행사	travel agency	**ADVERB**	
예약(하다)	reservation	곧	right away, soon
오랫동안	for a long time	약	approximately
왕복	round-trip	혼자	alone
외국	foreign country	**SUFFIX**	
장학금	scholarship	~(으)면 되다	all one needs is
짐	luggage, load	~게 되다	turn out that
출발(하다)	departure		
편도	one-way trip		
표	ticket		

NEW EXPRESSIONS

1. 그럴게요 means 'I will do so', which is an abbreviated form of 그렇게 할게요.

2. 필요하다 'to need, be necessary' has two ways of negation such as 필요 없다 'to be unnecessary' and 안 필요하다 'to not need'. However, there is no expression 필요 있다.

GRAMMAR

G3.1   ~게 되다: change or turn of events

Examples

(1)   A: 요즘 뭐 하세요?   What are you doing these days?
       B: 다음 달부터 학교   It turned out that I am going to
             도서관에서 일하**게**   work in the school library starting
             됐어요.   next month.

(2)   A: 저 이번에 장학금을   I got offered a scholarship.
             받**게 됐어요**.   (Lit., It turned out that I will
                                      receive a scholarship.)
       B: 그래요? 잘 됐네요.   Is that right? That's great.

(3)   외국어를 배우면 외국 문화를 더 잘 이해하**게 될 거예요**.

(4)   A: 다음 달에 동생이랑 서울에 가는 거 맞지요?
       B: 사실은 저 혼자 먼저 떠나**게 됐어요**.

Notes

1. 되다 literally means 'become' or 'turn out'. ~게 되다, literally meaning 'turn out to ~', 'come to ~', or 'get to ~', expresses a change in situation or turn of events. That is, a person was in one event and is now in another event. The change in situation or turn of events is mostly accidental or something that is independent of the person's will or volition. It is typically used in telling news.

2. ~게 되다 is mostly used with verbs.

3. ~게 되다 is compared with ~어지다 (G1.1), which combines mostly with adjectives and expresses a change of state.

             날씨가 갑자기 추워졌어요.   It's become cold suddenly.
             요즘은 일찍 어두워져요.   It gets dark earlier these days.

Exercises

1. Indicate in Korean the changes in situation or turn of events that occurred in the given description.

> (1)   I was admitted to graduate school, and so I will be attending graduate school this fall semester.
>
>   이번 가을에 대학원에 가게 됐어요.
>
> (2)   I didn't like sports before, but now I like them.
>
>   _____
>
> (3)   If you leave now, you will arrive around 6 o'clock.
>
>   _____
>
> (4)   Michael cannot come because he is busy now, but later he will come.
>
>   _____
>
> (5)   I was going to study Korean here in America this summer. But it turned out that I get to go to Seoul to see Steve as well as to study Korean.
>
>   _____

2. State the changes of events that occurred as a result of the given events.

> (1)   [서울에서 부산까지 기차로 5시간 걸려요. 지금 4시예요.]
>
>   지금 출발하면 부산에 9시에 도착하게 돼요/될 거예요.
>
> (2)   A: 한국어를 얼마나 배우면 뉴스를 알아 듣게 돼요?
>
>   B: 약 2년만 배우면 _____
>
>   (You will get to understand.)
>
> (3)   손을 다쳤어요.
>
>   그래서 한 달동안 _____
>
>   (I will not be able to play basketball.)
>
> (4)   서울에 있는 한국어 여름 학교에서 장학금을 받았어요.
>
>   그래서 이번 여름에 _____

(5)   한국에 있는 친구들을 오랫동안 못 만났어요.

　　　그런데, 이번에 한국에 가면 ＿＿＿＿＿＿＿＿＿＿＿＿

　　　　　　　　　　　　　　　　　　　(I will get to see them.)

(6)   여행 가방이 너무 무거워요. 그래서 공항에서 돈을 더

　　　＿＿＿＿＿＿＿＿＿＿＿＿.

G3.2   ~(으)면 되다 'have only to . . .', 'all one needs is . . .'

Examples

(1)   A: 여행 준비 다 했어요?   Did you prepare everything
　　　　　　　　　　　　　　　　　　for your trip?

　　　B: 네, 비자는 지난주에 받았고,   Yes, I got my visa last week,
　　　　　　이젠 짐만 싸**면 돼요**.   and now I have only to pack
　　　　　　　　　　　　　　　　　　my luggage.

(2)   A: 한국 가는 비행기 표   How much is the air ticket to
　　　　　　얼마예요?   Korea?

　　　B: 편도는 1,000불인데,   One-way is $1,000, but all
　　　　　　왕복은 1,200불만 내**면**   you need to pay for round-
　　　　　　돼요/ 주시**면 돼요**.   trip is $1,200.

(3)   A: 여기 화장실이 어디예요?

　　　B: 저기 가운데 건물에서 왼쪽으로 가시**면 돼요**.

(4)   국내선은 3층, 국제선은 1층으로 가시**면 됩니다**.

Notes

1. ~(으)면 되다, literally meaning 'It would do if . . .' or 'It would be all right/good if . . .', is used to tell what is needed to resolve a given situation.

2. N만 ~(으)면 되다 emphasizes the minimum that it takes to resolve the given situation. It is best translated as 'all I have to do is'.

Exercises

1. Complete the following sentences.

(1)   한국어를 잘하고 싶으면 <u>한국 친구를 사귀면 돼요</u>.

(2)   인터넷에서 무료로 책을 읽고 싶으면 _____

(3)   길을 잘 모르면 _____

(4)   전화번호를 모르면 _____

(5)   도서관에서 음악을 들으려면 _____

(6)   비행기 표를 예약하고 싶으면 여행사에 _____

2. Using ~(으)면 돼요 or N만 ~(으)면 돼요, complete the following dialogues, providing a resolution to the given situation.

(1)   A: 비행기 표 언제까지 사야 돼요?

       B: 예약은 하셨죠?

             <u>그럼 떠나기 2주 전까지만 사시면 돼요</u>.

(2)   A: 여행 준비 다 됐어요?

       B: 네, 이제 _____

(3)   A: 숙제할 게 많아요?

       B: 아니요, _____

(4)   A: 공항까지 직접 운전하실 거예요?

       B: 아니요, 시청에서 공항버스를 _____

(5)   A: 한국어를 잘하고 싶은데, 어떻게 하면 좋을까요?

       B: _____

Conversation 2 ｜ 한국에 갔다 왔어요.

(소피아가 여름 방학이 끝나고 다시 학교에 돌아왔습니다.)

유미:　　　소피아 씨, 방학 때 어디 갔었어요? G3.3

소피아:　　네, 한국에 갔다 왔어요.

유미:　　　그랬어요? 좋았겠네요.

소피아:　　네, 정말 볼 것도 많고 재미있었어요. 여행하는
　　　　　　동안 맛있는 음식도 먹고 구경도 많이 했어요.

유미:　　　어디가 제일 좋았어요?

소피아:　　여러 군데 다녔는데 제주도하고 경주가
　　　　　　제일 기억에 남아요.

유미:　　　저도 어렸을 때 경주에 가 본 적이G3.4 있어요.
　　　　　　그런데 제주도는 못 가 봤어요.

소피아:　　그래요? 제주도도 정말 멋있으니까G3.5 나중에
　　　　　　꼭 한번 가 보세요.

COMPREHENSION QUESTIONS

1. 소피아는 방학 동안 무슨 일을 했습니까?
2. 소피아가 한국에서 여행한 곳 중에서 어디가 제일 기억에 남습니까?
3. 유미는 언제 경주에 가 보았습니까?

NEW WORDS

NOUN		ADJECTIVE	
걱정(하다)	worry, concern	기쁘다	to be joyful, glad
경주	Gyeongju	멋있다	to be stylish, cool
경치	scenery, view	아름답다	to be beautiful
기억(하다)	memory	유명하다	to be famous
남	south	인상적이다	to be impressive
동	east	**VERB**	
바다	sea	남다	to remain
박물관	museum	다니다	to get around
북	north	다녀오다	to go and get back
서	west	풀다	to relieve
섬	island	**ADVERB**	
스트레스	stress	아까	a while ago
옛날	the old days	주로	mostly, mainly
절	Buddhist temple	하나도	(not) at all
제주도	Jeju Island	**SUFFIX**	
호텔	hotel	~(으)니까	expresses reason
INTERJECTION		~어/아 본 적(이)	expresses past
와	wow	있다/없다	experience
		~었었/았었/ㅆ었	remote past

NEW EXPRESSIONS

1. 군데 'place' is used as a counter for numeric expressions (한 군데, 열 군데, 여러 군데). Compare this with 장소 'place' which is an independent noun, and with 곳 or 데 'place', which has to be used with a modifying expression (이런 데, 저런 곳, 재미있는 데, 좋은 곳).

2. 갔다 오다 means 'to go and come back' as in:

학교에 갔다 왔어요.   I came back home from school.
작년에 한국에 갔다 왔어요. I visited Korea last year.

GRAMMAR

G3.3	Doubling of ~었-: ~었었-/~았었-/~써었-

Examples

(1)   민지: 방학 때 어디로 여행 **갔었**어요?
       마크: 제주도로 갔었어요.
       민지: 와, 재미있었겠네요!

(2)   제니: 마크 어디 갔어요?
       샌디: 커피 마시러 갔어요.
               (잠시 후에 마크가 돌아왔습니다)
       제니: 마크 씨, 어디 **갔었**어요?
       마크: 커피 마시러 **갔었**어요.

(3)   유미: 유진 씨, 스티브 씨 일어났어요?
       유진: 네, 일어났어요.
       유미: 마크 씨는요?
       유진: 아까 일어**났었**어요. 그런데 또 자요.

(4)   유미: 마크 씨 피아노 잘 쳐요?
       마크: 어렸을 때는 좀 **쳤었**는데 지금은 못 쳐요.

Notes

1. The doubling of ~었- (realized as ~었었-, ~았었- or ~써었-) is used in focusing on a past event whose effect is no longer relevant at the present moment. In (1), for example, Mark is now back, and the effect of his being gone is no longer felt. The use of single ~었- in this context could mean that Mark is still in 제주도. The same is true with (2).

2. Similarly in (3) and (4), ~었었- expresses a past situation that does not continue or is not true any more. More examples are given below:

> 옛날에는 한국에 호랑이가 많았었어요. 지금은 호랑이가 없어요.
> 어렸을 때는 매일 공원에 놀러 갔었어요. 지금은 자주 못 가요.

3. In English, however, sometimes both single and double ~었- are translated in the same way, as in (3).

Exercise

Complete the dialogues using ~었었-.

(1)　유미:　방학 때 뭐 했어요?

　　　샌디:　[I went to Korea to study Korean.]

　　　　　　한국어 배우러 한국에 갔었어요.

(2)　A:　방학 때 뭐 했어요?

　　　B:　_____

　　　　　[I went to Chicago to see a friend.]

(3)　A:　_____

　　　　　[Did you go to the party yesterday?]

　　　B:　아니요, 바빠서 못 갔어요.

(4)　A:　요즘 야구장에 자주 가세요?

　　　B:　_____

　　　　　[No. I used to go to the baseball stadium often
　　　　　but I haven't been able to go recently at all.]

(5)　A:　민수는 그렇게 노래를 못 불러요?

　　　B:　_____

　　　　　[He used to sing well . . . (I don't know why not
　　　　　now.)]

(6)　A:　지금 밖에 날씨가 어때요?

　　　B:　_____

　　　　　[It was windy a while ago, but now it is all right.]

(7)　A:　보통 어떤 운동을 하세요?

　　　B:　_____

　　　　　[I used to swim every day, but I just jog these days.]

G3.4 ~어/아 본 적(이) 있다/없다 'there has been an/no occasion of . . .'

Examples

(1)   A: 유럽에 <u>가 봤어요</u>?   Have you ever been
                                                                 to Europe?

        B: 네, 옛날에 **가 본 적이 있어요**.   Yes, I've been there
               박물관이 인상적이었어요.   in the past.

(2)   A: 제주도에 여행**가 본 적 있어요**?   Have you ever
                                                                 visited Jeju Island?

        B: 아니요, 못 <u>가 봤어요</u>.   No, I haven't.
        A: 제주도는 한국에서 가장 경치가
               아름답고 유명한 섬이에요.
               동서남북 어디에 가도 정말 멋있어요.

(3)   A: 스티브 윌슨 아세요?
        B: 이름은 들어 봤는데 아직   His name sounds familiar,
               만**나 본 적은 없어요**.   but I haven't met him yet.

Notes

1. Recall that ~어/아 보다 in the past tense (~어 봤어요) expresses a past experience, as underlined in (1) and (2). Also recall that ~(으)ㄴ 적이 있다 means '[As I recall] there has been an occasion of . . .' Together, ~어/아 본 적이 있다/없다 means 'There has been an/no occasion in which one has an/no experience of . . .' In questions, it is more appropriately translated as 'Have you ever . . .?', as in (2).

2. The experience mentioned must be one retrieved out of long-term memory. It is usually accompanied by a time expression such as 작년에 'last year', 몇 달 전에 'a few months ago', or even 얼마 전에 'some time ago'. It would not be appropriate, however, to respond to the question 야구장에 가 본 적 있어요? with 지난 주에 가 본 적이 있어요, because it is too recent. It is not something to retrieve from long-term memory, but is in the speaker's current memory.

3. When the verb 보다 is used with ~어/아 본 적이 있다/없다 construction,

V.S. ~어/아 part is omitted as in 본 적이 있다/없다. There is no such expression as 봐 본 적이 있다/없다.

Exercise

Answer the given questions using the ~이/아 본적이 있다/없다 structure.

(1) A: 절에 가 봤어요?

  B: <u>네, 한국에서 가 본 적이 있어요.</u>

(2) A: 오페라(opera) 들어 봤어요?

  B: _____

(3) A: 알래스카(Alaska)에 가 봤어요?

  B: _____

(4) A: 한복 입어 봤어요?

  B: _____

(5) A: 골프 쳐 봤어요?

  B: _____

(6) A: 스키 타 봤어요?

  B: _____

G3.5	~(으)니까: expressing a reason or logical sequence

Examples

[Expressing reason]

(1) A: 비가 많이 오**니까**   Because it's raining a lot,
       운전할 때 조심하세요.   please drive carefully.

  B: 네, 걱정하지 마세요.

(2) A: 같이 점심 먹으러 갈래요?

  B: 저는 좀 전에 먹었으**니까** 수지 씨랑 같이 가세요.

(3) 시간이 없**으니까**   Since we don't have much
   택시를 타고 갈까요?   time, shall we go by taxi?

[Temporal sequence]
(4)   소연: 주로 무슨 운동을 해요?
        성희: 요즘은 수영 배우고 있어요.
               해 보**니까** 스트레스를   When I tried swimming,
               풀 수 있어서 좋아요.   I found that it relieves stress.

(5)   A: 어제 일찍 잤어요?
        B: 아니요, 어제 집에 들어가**니까** 벌써 밤 12시였어요.

Notes

1. In examples (1) – (3), ~(으)니까 specifies a reason or ground for why the subsequent message is said. By appealing to a reason that is obvious or familiar to the listener, the speaker justifies and strengthens the validity of what is said subsequently. ~(으)니까 is conveniently translated as 'since', 'now that', 'given that', and 'because'.

2. It is frequently used in giving an excuse, explanation, or justification for a command or request to make your command sound more convincing and persuasive as in examples (1) – (3).

3. In examples (4) and (5), ~(으)니까 expresses a temporal sequence; that is, one situation temporally follows another. With A~(으)니까 B, the speaker's viewpoint is at the time of the occurrence of event A so that the speaker witnesses the occurrence of event B, as if the speaker follows through these events. That is to say, the two events are not just sequentially connected, but connected through the speaker's experience because event A leads the speaker to witness or experience event B.

4. It should be noted that ~(으)니까 in (4) and (5) is not marked for time even when it refers to a past event. This is because the speaker is describing the two sequential events as if he/she is currently witnessing them as he/she follows through the events.

Exercises

1. Using the ~(으)니까 form, complete the discourse.

(1)   A: 뭐 타고 갈까요?

        B: <u>지금 시간에는 길이 막히니까</u> 지하철을 타요.

(2)   A: 저, 시간 있으면 오늘 좀 만날 수 있을까요?

        B: _____ 내일 만나면 안 될까요?

        A: 네, 그럼 내일 봐요.

(3)   A: 이 선생님 계세요?

        B: _____ 이따가 오후에 오세요.

(4)   A: 거기까지 가는 버스 있어요?

        B: 직접 가는 _____ 지하철을 타세요.

(5)   A: 한국에 언제 가세요?

        B: _____ 일주일 후에 가요.

(6)   A: 저한테서 빌린 비디오 언제 돌려 주실 거예요?

        B: _____ 다음 주에 돌려 드릴게요.

2. Using ~(으)니까, provide an event that leads to witnessing the given situation.

(1)   A: 언니한테 전화했어요?

        B: 네.

        A: 언니가 좋아했겠네요.

        B: 네. <u>오랜만에 전화하니까</u> 언니가 너무 기뻐했어요.

(2)   소연: 민지 씨, 어디 아파요?

        민지: 아니요, 시험 때문에 매일 늦게까지 책을

                _____ 좀 피곤해요.

(3)   성희: 소연 씨, 요즘 굉장히 좋아 보여요.

        소연: 네. 요즘 매일 수영해요.

                _____ 스트레스도 풀 수 있고

                몸이 가벼워져서 참 좋아요.

(4)   A: 성희 씨 만났어요? 아까 도서관에서 찾던데요.

        B: 아니요, 못 만났어요. _____ 벌써

                가고 없었어요.

Narration   소피아의 한국 여행

저는 한국에 있는 동안 경주와 제주도에 다녀왔습니다.
경주는 옛날 신라의 수도입니다. 한국에는 절이 많이
있는데, 경주의 불국사가 가장 유명하고 아름답습니다.
특히 소피아는 불국사에 있는 다보탑과 석가탑이
인상적이었습니다.
제주도는 한국에서 가장 큰 섬입니다. 서울에서 비행기로
한 시간 정도 걸립니다. 제주도는 남쪽에 있어서
날씨가 따뜻하고 경치가 아름답습니다. 저는 여러 곳을
구경했는데, 그 중에서 섬 가운데에 있는 한라산이 가장
마음에 들었습니다. 참 즐거운 여행이었습니다.

다보탑 'Dabo Tower'
불국사 'Bulguksa'
석가탑 'Seokga Tower'
석굴암 'Seokguram'
수도   'capital city'
신라   'Silla'
한라산 'Halla Mount'

COMPREHENSION QUESTIONS

1. 소피아는 한국에서 어디로 여행을 갔습니까?
2. 불국사는 어떤 곳입니까?
3. 어느 곳이 가장 인상적이었습니까?
4. 서울에서 제주도까지 얼마나 걸립니까?
5. 제주도는 어떤 곳입니까?

NEW EXPRESSIONS

인상적 'impressive' consists of 인상 'impression' and the suffix ~적. Some Sino-Korean nouns take the suffix ~적, whose meaning is similar to "~ive" or "~ic" in English, and have the following pattern.

Adjective		Modifier	Adverb
인상적이다	to be impressive	인상적인	인상적으로
적극적이다	to be positive	적극적인	적극적으로
소극적이다	to be passive	소극적인	소극적으로

CULTURE

경주: **The ancient capital of the Silla Kingdom**

경주는 역사가 아주 오래된 도시입니다. 경주는 기원전(B.C.) 57년부터 서기(A.D.) 935년까지 신라의 수도였습니다. 신라는 오래 전에 한반도(Korean Peninsula)에 있던 세 나라 중 하나입니다. 신라는 과학, 문화, 예술이 발달하였습니다. 경주에는 신라 시대의 불교 문화 예술과 건축물들이 지금까지도 많이 남아있습니다.

UNESCO (United Nations Educational,

Scientific, and Cultural Organization)는 2000년에 '경주 역사 유적 지구 (Gyeongju Historic Areas)'를 '세계 유산(World Heritage Site)'으로 지정하였습니다. 특히 불국사와 석굴암은 신라 시대의 아름답던 불교 문화를 보여 주는 건축물로 아주 유명합니다. 경주에는 별과 하늘을 볼 수 있는 아시아에서 가장 오래된 건축물인 첨성대도 있습니다. 경주는 도시가 하나의 박물관 같습니다.

건축물	building, structure	석굴	stone cave
과학	science	수도	capital city
남아 있다	to remain	시대	period
발달(하다)	development	아시아	Asia
불교	Buddhism	예술	art
별	star	지정하다	to appoint
사찰	temple	특히	particularly

USAGE

1. Calling a travel agency and buying an airline ticket

Examples

(샌디가 비행기 표를 예약하려고 여행사에 전화합니다.)

직원: 여행사입니다.
샌디: 여보세요.
　　　저, 서울 가는 비행기표 좀 예약하고 싶은데요.
직원: 몇 분이 가십니까?
샌디: 한 사람인데요.
직원: 언제 떠나십니까?
샌디: 6월 2일에 출발해서 7월 31일에 돌아오려고 하는데요.
　　　왕복에 얼마예요?
직원: 1350불입니다. 예약해 드릴까요?
샌디: 네. 예약해 주세요.
직원: 성함하고 카드 번호 좀 불러 주시겠어요?
샌디: 네. (잠시 후)
직원: 출발 1주일 전에 오셔서 티켓 찾아가시면 됩니다.
샌디: 고맙습니다.

(1) Making a reservation

_____(Destination) 가는 비행기표 예약하려는데요/예약했으면 하는데요.

(2) Giving departure and return dates

____ 월 _____일에 출발해서 _____월 _____일에 돌아오려고 하는데요.
(Departure date)　　　　　　　(Return date)

(3) Asking about airfare

　　　_____ (airline)은/는 얼마예요?
대한항공은 얼마예요　　　　　How much is Korean Airline (KAL)?
(항공료가) 얼마예요?　　　　　How much is the airfare?
값은 어떻게 돼요?　　　　　　What's the fare?

(4) Choosing an airline

> A: 어느 항공편 이용하시겠습니까?
>   어느 비행기요? or 어느 비행기로 가시겠습니까?
>   Which airline would you like to use?
> B: _____(name of an airline)(으)로 해 주세요.

Useful words

편도 one-way, 항공료 airfare, 출발 departure, 도착 arrival, 항공편 an airline, 좌석 a seat, 창가 좌석 a window seat, 항공권/티켓/비행기표 an airline ticket, 일등석 a first class (seat), 일반석 an economy class (seat)

[Exercise 1] (Role-play) Make a dialogue between a customer and a travel agent for the following situations:

> (1)   Customer wants to reserve two round-trip plane tickets from Seoul to Chicago.

> (2)   Customer wants to buy a one-way plane ticket from New York to Seoul.

2. Talking about vacation and summer jobs

Examples

샌디 : 영미 씨, 오래간만이에요.
       여름 방학 잘 보냈어요?
영미: 백화점에서 아르바이트 (part-time job) 했어요.
샌디: 무슨 아르바이트 했어요?
영미: 백화점에서 일했어요.
       샌디씨는 방학 때 어디 다녀 왔어요?
샌디: 한국에 갔다 왔어요.
영미: 그랬어요? 재미있었어요?
샌디: 네, 근데 날씨 때문에 좀 고생했어요.
영미: 왜요? 날씨가 어땠는데요?
샌디: 한국 여름 날씨가 너무 더웠어요.

[Exercise 1]   Converse with your partner regarding the past summer vacation.

[Exercise 2]   Exchange the following information with your classmates. Write down the answers and report them to the class.

(1)   여름 방학 동안 아르바이트 해 본 적 있으세요?

(2)   왜 아르바이트 했어요?

(3)   어디서 일했어요?

(4)   무슨 일을 했어요?

(5)   일주일에 몇 시간 일했어요?

(6)   얼마나 벌었어요?

(7)   앞으로 어떤 아르바이트를 하고 싶으세요?

[Exercise 3] 가장 기억에 남는 여행에 대해서 (about) 얘기해 보세요.

3. Describing past events

Examples

(1)   A: 여름 방학 때 어디 갔다 왔어요?
       B: 한국에 갔다 왔어요.
       A: 그랬어요? 한국에 얼마 동안 있었어요?
       B: 두 달 있었어요.
       A: 한국에 있는 동안 여행 많이 했어요?
       B: 네, 여러 군데 다녔어요.
       A: 재미있었겠네요. 어디가 제일 좋았어요?
       B: 경주가 제일 인상적이었어요.

(2)   지난 여름 방학 동안 한국에 갔다 왔어요. 6월 말에 가서 8월 30일에 미국에 돌아왔어요. 한국에 가 본 적이 없었기 때문에 처음에는 약간 걱정이 됐어요. 서울에서 두 달 동안 한국어를 배웠는데 참 재미있었어요. 한국에 있는 동안 친구들도 많이 사귀었어요.

친구들하고 여행도 많이 했어요. 부산에도 가고 경주에도
놀러 갔어요. 내년 여름에도 한국에 가고 싶어요.
(걱정이 됐어요 was worried)

[Exercise 1] Take the roles of 영미 and 샌디.

영미: _____?

샌디: 서울에 갔다 왔어요.

영미: _____?

샌디: 한국어 배우러 갔어요.

영미: _____?

샌디: 여러 군데 갔어요.

영미: _____?

샌디: 경주가 제일 좋았어요.

영미: _____?

샌디: 지난 주말에 돌아왔어요.

[Exercise 2] Pair up and look at your schedule book for the past summer.
Ask each other questions about your activities during the past summer.

[Exercise 3] Converse with your partner about your and his/her past
experiences in the following areas.

(1)   외국 여행 경험

(2)   아르바이트 경험 (experience)

(3)   가장 기억에 남는 생일 파티/선물

(4)   가장 인상적인 선생님

[Exercise 4] Write a letter to your Korean teacher about your most recent
summer vacation and read it to the class.

4. Skimming newspaper ads for airline tickets and travel information

(Sandy is looking for a round-trip airline ticket from New York to Seoul and is reading the following ads in a Korean newspaper.)

뉴서울 여행사

뉴욕-서울행 항공권 특별 세일 $799
미국-한국 왕복 가장 싼 가격
미국 국내선 가장 싼 가격
유럽, 남미, 동남아 전세계 비행기표
서울 출발 미국행 비행기표
서울, 동남아, 미국 내 호텔 예약 할인
전화 (800) 790-4236

티켓 무료 배달해 드립니다.

(국내선 domestic airline, 남미 South America, 동남아 Southeast Asia, 할인 a discount, 무료 배달 free delivery)

[Exercise 1] Make a telephone conversation with a travel agent (your partner) based on the ad.

[Exercise 2] Read the ad above and mark the following statements as T(rue) or F(alse).

(1)　The 뉴서울 travel agency offers a special sale price for round-trip tickets from New York to Seoul. _____

(2)　The travel agency also arranges hotel reservations. _____

(3)　There will be a charge for ticket delivery. _____

(4)　The travel agency offers a special sale price for tickets from Seoul to the United States. _____

Lesson 3. Travel

CONVERSATION 1: It turned out that I am going to Korea.

(Sophia met Michael at the campus of New York University.)

Michael:	How are you, Sophia. Where are you going?
Sophia:	Oh, Michael, I was going to call you. I met you just in time.
Michael:	Why?
Sophia:	In fact, it turned out that I'm going to Korea this summer.
Michael:	Is that so? Good for you. By the way, Steve is in Seoul. If you meet him, please say hi to him.
Sophia:	Yes, I will.
Michael:	Did you buy the flight ticket?
Sophia:	Yes, I already made a reservation.
Michael:	How much is the round-trip to Korea?
Sophia:	It's 1,600 dollars.
Michael:	You don't need a visa?
Sophia:	No. Just a passport will be okay.

CONVERSATION 2: I have been to Korea.

(Sophia returned to school after summer vacation.)

Yumi:	Sophia, have you been anywhere during the vacation?
Sophia:	Yes, I have been to Korea.
Yumi:	Was that so? It must have been nice.
Sophia:	Yes, there were so many things to see and it was fun. While I was traveling I ate delicious foods, and I went sightseeing a lot.
Yumi:	Which place did you like most?
Sophia:	I went to many places. Jeju Island and Gyeongju are the most memorable.
Yumi:	I have been to Gyeongju when I was young, but I have never been to Jeju Island.
Sophia:	Is that so? Definitely visit Jeju Island because it is also great.

NARRATION: Sophia's trip to Korea

I have been to Gyeongju and to Jeju Island during my stay in Korea. Gyeongju is the capital city of old Silla. There are many temples in Korea, but Bulguksa in Gyeongju is the most famous and beautiful. Dabo Tower and Seokga Tower at Bulguksa were especially impressive to me.

Jeju Island is the biggest island in Korea. It takes about one hour from Seoul to get there by airplane. Since Jeju Island is on the southern end, the weather is warm. Also, the scenery is beautiful. I went sightseeing at several places. Among them, I liked Halla Mount in the middle of the island. It was a very pleasant trip.

CULTURE: 경주

Gyeongju is a city with a very long history. Gyeongju was the capital city of Silla from 57 B.C. to A.D 935. Silla is one of the three kingdoms that existed on the Korean Peninsula a long time ago. Silla had advanced science, culture, and art. Many artifacts of Buddhist culture and architecture of Silla can still be seen in Gyeongju.

UNESCO (United Nations Educational, Scientific, and Cultural Organization) designated the Gyeongju Historic Areas as a World Heritage Site in 2000. Bulguksa and Seokguram have very famous architecture that shows the beautiful Buddhist culture of Silla. There is the oldest architecture in Asia, from which you can see the stars and the sky. Gyeongju is a city that is like a museum.

4과 한국 생활 I   [Life in Korea I]

Conversation 1	인사동에 가는 길이에요.

(민지는 기숙사 입구에서 우진이를 우연히 만났습니다.)

민지: 우진 씨, 어디 가세요?

우진: 선물 사러 인사동에 가는 길이에요.^{G4.1}

민지: 왜요?

우진: 이 달 말이 엄마 생신이거든요.^{G4.2}

민지: 아, 그래요? 뭘 사실 건데요?

우진: 수저 세트를 살까 해요.

민지: 그거 좋은 생각이네요. 인사동에 가면 한국
전통 공예품 가게들이 많으니까 마음에 드는
걸 살 수 있을 거예요.

우진: 혹시 지금 시간이 되면 저하고 같이 가실래요?

민지: 네, 같이 가요. 그런데 가는 길에 은행에서
돈을 찾아야 되는데.

우진: 네, 그러세요.

COMPREHENSION QUESTIONS

1. 우진이는 왜 선물을 사려고 합니까?
2. 우진이는 무엇을 사고 싶어합니까?
3. 우진이와 민지는 왜 인사동에서 선물을 사려고 합니까?
4. 민지는 가는 길에 무엇을 하려고 합니까?

NEW WORDS

NOUN		학비	tuition
계좌	account	**VERB**	
공예품	handicraft item	바빠지다	to get busier
길	way, street	생기다	to be formed
몸	body	잊다	to forget
병원	hospital	졸리다	to feel sleepy
성적	grade	(돈을) 찾다	to withdraw money
세트	a set	익숙하다	to be familiar
소포	parcel	**ADJECTIVE**	
수저	spoon and chopsticks	편안하다	to be comfortable
숟가락	spoon	**ADVERB**	
신분증	identification card	우연히	by chance
유학생	student abroad	항상	always
인사동	Insadong	혹시	by any chance
전통	tradition	**SUFFIX**	
젓가락	chopsticks	~거든요	you see (because)
직원	staff, employee	~는 길이다	(be) on one's way
하루 종일	all day		

NEW EXPRESSIONS

1. 수저 is a combination of 숟가락 'spoon' and 젓가락 'a pair of chopsticks'.

2. 시간이 되다 'to have enough time, to be available' as in 이번 주말에 시간이 되세요? 'Are you available this weekend?'

3. 돈을 찾다 means 'to withdraw money' from a bank account. 돈을 빼다 'to remove, take out' is used instead if you withdraw cash from an ATM.

GRAMMAR

G4.1 ~는 길이다/~는 길에 '(be) on one's way'

Examples

(1)   A: 어디 가세요?   Where are you going?
       B: 소포 부치러 우체국에 I'm on my way to the post office
             가**는 길이에요**.   to mail this package.

(2)   A: 어디 가세요?
       B: 몸이 아파서 병원에 가**는 길이에요**.

(3)   A: 오늘 은행에 갈 거예요?
       B: 네, 이따가 오후에 갈 건데요.
       A: 그럼 은행 갔다 오**는 길에** 주스 좀 사 올래요?
       B: 그럴게요.

Notes

1. 길 literally means 'a way, a road, a street'. Combined with a movement verb like 가다, 오다, 갔다 오다, ~는 길에 means 'on one's way (back from/ to)'. ~는 길이에요 means '. . . is on one's way'.

    . . . 에 가는/오는 길에   on one's way to/back to . . .
    . . . 에서 오는 길에   on one's way back from . . .

2. In the original usage of ~는 길에/~는 길이에요, one is in the middle of going or coming to/from a location, as in (1) and (2). The expression, however, can also be used to mean 'since one is going to . . .', as in (3).

Exercises

1. Two people run into each other. Using ~는 길이에요, answer each question with the given location.

    (1)   A: 어디 가세요?

           B: [school] 학교 가는 길이에요.

(2) A: 어디 가세요?

B: [library] _____

(3) A: 어디 갔다 오세요?

B: [a store] _____

(4) (학교에서 수업이 다 끝났습니다.)

A: 집에 가세요?

B: [home] 네, _____

(5) A: 지금 학교에서 오세요?

B: 아니요, [a friend's house] _____

2. You would like to ask your friend to do something for you on his/her way (back) from/to some place. Make up your request based on the given information.

(1) 민지: 우진 씨, 우체국 안 가요?

우진: 아, 잊어 버렸어요. 오후에 가야겠네요.

민지: 그럼, 우체국 가는 길에 빵 좀 사 줄래요? [빵]

우진: 그럴게요.

(2) A: 어디 가세요?

B: 집 앞에 있는 가게에 가요.

A: 그럼, _____ [편지/부치다]

(3) A: 어디 가세요?

B: 책 빌리러 도서관에 가요.

A: 그럼, _____ [물/사다]

(4) A: 어디 가세요?

B: 소포 부치러 우체국에 가는 길이에요.

A: 그럼, _____ [책/빌려 오다]

G4.2   ~거든요 'you see, (because)~'

Examples

(1)   A: 요즘 많이 바빠졌네요.
        B: 네, 주말에는 하루 종일 일해요.
        A: 왜요?
        B: 학비가 많이 올랐**거든요**.

(2)   학생: 은행 계좌 만들고 싶은데요.
        직원: 신분증 좀 주시겠어요?
        학생: 제가 유학생이**거든요**. 여권도 괜찮을까요?
        직원: 그럼요.

(3)   (at a restaurant table)
        A: 여기 두 명 더 오**거든요**.
              숟가락, 젓가락 좀 더 갖다 주시겠어요?
        B: 네. 금방 갖다 드릴게요.

(4)   A: 한국 생활이 어떠세요?
        B: 많이 편안해졌어요.
              이제는 한국 문화에 익숙하**거든요**.

Notes

1. The ~거든요 sentence often provides a reason or explanation why the situation currently at issue is the way it is.

2. The reason or explanation provided must be something that the listener would understand easily when he/she hears it. ~거든요 is used when the speaker expects the listener to easily recognize the correlation between the situation currently at issue and the reason/explanation provided. It is roughly equivalent to saying in English 'You see, (because) . . .'

Exercises

1. Make up a response that explains the situation currently at issue.

(1)   A: 왜 기분이 안 좋으세요?

         B: <u>시험을 잘 못 봤거든요.</u>

(2)   A: 봄 방학 때 집에 안 가세요?

         B: 못 가요. _____

(3)   A: 왜 한국어를 배우세요?

         B: _____

(4)   A: 무슨 비행기로 가세요?

         B: 항상 대한항공(Korean Air)으로 가요.

               _____

(5)   A: (수영장에서) 왜 수영 안 하세요?

         B: _____

(6)   A: 저 이번에 장학금을 받게 됐어요.

         B: 그래요? 어떻게 받았어요?

         A: 성적이 _____

2. Make up a question that is appropriate for the given context.

(1)   A: <u>많이 졸리세요?</u>

         B: 네, 어제 잠을 세 시간밖에 못 잤거든요.

(2)   A: _____?

         B: 한국 친구가 생겼거든요.

(3)   A: _____?

         B: 얼굴이 예쁘거든요.

(4)   A: _____?

         B: 저하고 별로 안 친하거든요.

(5)   A: _____?

         B: 오늘 저녁에 파티가 있거든요.

(6)   A: _____?

         B: 방이 너무 좁아서 불편하거든요.

Conversation 2 | 소포를 부치려고 하는데요.

(우진이가 미국에 소포를 부치려고 우체국에 갔습니다.)

직원: 어서 오세요. 어떻게 도와 드릴까요?

우진: 미국으로 소포를 부치려고 하는데

         얼마나 걸릴까요?

직원: 미국 어디요?G4.3

우진: 뉴욕이요.

직원: 사흘 정도 걸려요.

우진: 그래요? 그 정도면 괜찮네요.

직원: 소포 안에 뭐가 들어 있어요?

         깨지기 쉬운 거예요?

우진: 아니에요. 수저 세트예요.

직원: (종이를 주면서) 소포 보내시려면G4.4

         여기에 주소 좀 적어 주세요.

우진: 네, 여기 있습니다. 수고하세요.

(우진이가 떠납니다.)

직원: 손님, 잠깐만요. 영수증 가져가셔야지요.^{G4.5}

우진: 아, 네. 감사합니다.

COMPREHENSION QUESTIONS

1. 우진이는 왜 우체국에 갔습니까?
2. 소포는 뉴욕까지 얼마나 걸립니까?
3. 우진이는 소포로 무엇을 부쳤습니까?

NEW WORDS

NOUN		VERB	
등기	registered mail	가져가다	to take, carry
보통	regular	깨지다	to break
봉투	envelope	도와 드리다*hon.*	to help
사흘	three days	들어 있다	to contain
상자	box	사용하다	to use
영수증	receipt	서다	to stand
우체통	postbox	적다	to write down
우편	mail	**ADJECTIVE**	
이틀	two days	똑같다	to be identical
적응(하다)	to adapt	비슷하다	to be similar
정도	approximate	정확하다	to be accurate
졸업식	commencement	친하다	to be close (to)
종이	paper	특별하다	to be special
주소	address	**SUFFIX**	
핸드폰	cellular phone	(이)요	It is [noun].
		~(으)려면	if . . . intends to
		~어/아야지요	expresses obligation

NEW EXPRESSIONS

1.   부치다 to mail   (편지를 부쳐요.)
      붙이다 to stick, affix   (봉투에 우표를 붙여요.)

2.   하루   one day   이틀   two days
      사흘   three days   나흘   four days

GRAMMAR

G4.3   N(이)요 'It is [noun].'

Examples

(1)   [우체국에서]
       직원: 상자 안에 뭐가 들어있어요?   What's in the box?
       우진: 옷**이요**. (옷 들어있어요./옷이에요.)   Clothes.

(2)   A: 어디까지 가세요?   How far are you
                                          going?
       B: 서울역**이요**. (서울역까지 가요.)   To Seoul Station.

(3)   A: 몇 학년이에요?   What year are you in?
       B: 일학년**이요**. (일학년이에요.)   Freshman/first year.

(4)   A: 전공이 뭐예요?   What is your major?
       B: 한국 역사**요**. (한국 역사예요.)   Korean history.

Notes

1. N(이)요 is used to give the simplest answer to a question by mentioning only the very item in question (underlined) without having to repeat whatever else is mentioned in the question. Compare this with the full answer provided in parentheses.

2. N이요 is used after a consonant, as in (1) – (3) and N요 after a vowel, as in (4). Speakers of some dialects may use 요 in both cases.

Exercise

Give the simplest answer to the given question.

(1) A: 무슨 운동을 좋아해요?

  B: <u>야구요</u>.

(2) A: 이거 누가 만들었어요?

  B: _____.

(3) A: 이번 학기에 한국어 누가 가르치세요?

  B: _____.

(4) A: 이거 등기로 하실래요, 보통으로 하실래요?

  B: _____.

(5) A: 어제 저녁에 뭐 먹었어요?

  B: _____.

(6) A: 어느 식당을 제일 좋아해요?

  B: _____.

G4.4 ~(으)려면 'if . . . intends to do'

Examples

(1) (우체국에서)
  손님: 우편으로 책을 보내**려면** 어떻게 해야 돼요?
  직원: 여기에 받는 사람 이름과 정확한 주소를 써 주세요.

(2) A: 한국 전통 공예품을 사**려면** 어디가 좋아요?
  B: 인사동에 가 보세요. 공예품을 많이 팔아요.

(3) A: 이거랑 똑같은 가방 있으세요?
  B: 똑같은 걸 사시**려면** 백화점에 가셔야 돼요
  A: 그러면 그냥 비슷한 걸로 주세요.

(4) 수업에 늦지 않**으려면** 밤에 일찍 자야 돼요.

Notes

1. Recall that ~(으)려고 하다 expresses that someone intends to do
something, and ~(으)면 is a conditional expression. Combined together
~(으)려면 means 'If one intends/plans/would like to . . .'
~(으)려면 is a contraction of ~(으)려고 하면.

2. The negation of ~(으)려면 is ~지 않으려면 as shown in (4).

Exercises

1. Complete the following sentences.

    (1)   소포를 부치려면 <u>우체국에 가야 돼요</u>.

    (2)   한국어를 잘하려면 _____

    (3)   건강해지려면 _____

    (4)   새 핸드폰을 사려면 _____

    (5)   친구한테 특별한 선물을 하려면 _____

    (6)   약속 시간에 늦지 않으려면 _____

    (7)   물건을 싸게 사려면 _____

    (8)   외국어를 배우려면 _____

2. Complete the following sentences using ~(으)려면.

    (1)   <u>학교에 9시까지 가려면</u> 집에서 8시에 떠나야 돼요.

    (2)   _____ 음식을 잘 먹어야 돼요.

    (3)   _____ 한국에 가야 돼요.

    (4)   _____ 우체국에 가야 돼요.

    (5)   _____ 지하철을 타야 돼요.

    (6)   _____ 우체통에 넣어야 돼요.

| G4.5 | ~어야/아야지요 'definitely/indeed/ought to/have to' |

Examples

(1)   A: 서 있지 말고 여기 앉아서 기다리세요.
      B: 아니요, 괜찮아요. 이제 그만 가**야지요**.

(2)   A: 오늘 밤 늦게까지 공부할 거예요?
      B: 아니요, 피곤한데 자**야지요**.

(3)   (Someone is helping you repair your computer. Since it is getting quite late, you know he/she must go, although you hope he/she would stay a bit longer.)

      You: 늦었는데 가 보셔**야지요**?
      Guest: 괜찮아요. 좀 더 있어도 돼요.

(4)   A: 한국에서 살기가 쉽지 않네요.
      B: 한국 생활에 빨리 적응하려면 친구를 많이 사귀**어야지요**.

Notes

1. ~어야/아야 refers to a person's obligation to do something or the necessity of a situation. ~지요 indicates the speaker's subjective judgment in the sense of 'indeed/certainly/ definitely/surely so', or 'of course'. Put together as ~어야/아야지요, the speaker shows his/her subjective judgment that the situation in question ought to happen.

2. It is often used in giving advice or a strong suggestion, as in (4).

Exercise

Complete the following dialogues using the ~어야/아야지요 form.

(1)   (In a crowded restaurant)
      A: 자리가 없네요.
      B: 예약 안 하셨어요? 주말에는 <u>예약을 하셔야지요</u>.

(2)   (A guest at your place is about to leave. It is a Korean

social norm to ask the guest to stay longer.)

Host: 왜 벌써 가시려고 하세요?

Guest: 너무 늦었는데 이제 그만 _____

(3)   A: 파티에 안 가세요?

B: 내일 시험이 있는데 _____

(4)   A: 민수 졸업식에 안 가세요?

B: 나하고 제일 친한 친구인데 _____

(5)   A: 밤 공기가 너무 차네요.

B: 문을 _____.

Narration   우진이의 편지

보고 싶은 엄마,

그동안 안녕하셨어요? 저는 몸 건강히 잘 지내고 있어요.
먼저 엄마 생신 축하 드려요. 한국에서 예쁜 수저 세트를
샀어요. 엄마 마음에 드셨으면 좋겠어요.

지난 번에 전화하셨을 때 제가 전화를 안 받아서 걱정
많이 하셨지요? 그 때 도서관에서 하루 종일 공부하고
있었어요. 이번 학기에 성적이 잘 나와서 장학금을 받게
됐어요. 학비는 안 보내 주셔도 돼요. 학교 생활에도 많이
적응했고 친구들도 많이 생겼어요. 그러니까 제 걱정은
하지 마세요. 그리고 항상 건강하세요. 가족들 모두 보고
싶어요.

그럼 또 연락 드릴게요. 안녕히 계세요.

2013년 6월 30일

서울에서
우진 올림

COMPREHENSION QUESTIONS

1. 이 편지는 누가 누구에게 보내는 것입니까?
2. 우진이는 어머니 생신에 무슨 선물을 드렸습니까?
3. 우진이는 어머니가 전화했을 때 어디에 있었습니까?
4. 우진이는 왜 학비를 안 받아도 됩니까?

CULTURE

인사동

한국의 전통 문화와 음식을 맛보려면 인사동에 꼭 가 봐야 합니다.
인사동은 서울 안국역에서 종로 2가까지 이르는 거리인데 한국의
전통 공예품과 골동품 가게들이 많은 곳입니다. 지하철 3호선을 타고
안국역에서 내려서 인사동으로 걸어가면 됩니다.

인사동에는 골동품과 공예품
가게들도 많지만 화랑, 전통 찻집,
전통 음식점들도 많습니다. 인사동
거리를 걸으면 공예품을 구경하는
학생들, 물건들을 고르는 외국인들,
전통 찻집에서 데이트를 하는
대학생들, 그리고 한식집에서 전통
음식을 드시는 할아버지, 할머니들을
볼 수 있습니다. 이렇게 인사동에는
볼거리와 먹거리가 많아서 나이 어린
학생들부터 할아버지, 할머니까지
그리고 외국인들도 모두 자주 가는
곳입니다. 한국의 전통 문화의
중심지인 인사동은 서울에서 꼭 가 볼 만한 곳입니다.

거리	street, avenue	전통 문화	traditional culture
골동품	antique	전통 찻집	traditional teahouse
공예품	craftwork	중심지	center (of)
맛보다	to taste	화랑	gallery
먹거리	things to eat	~(으)ㄹ 만한	worthy of
볼거리	things to watch	~까지 이르다	reach to

USAGE

1. Using postal services

Examples

(1)   (Sending mail and packages at the post office)
        A: 소포 부치려고 하는데요.
        B: 어디 보내실 거예요?
        A: 부산에 보내려고요.
        B: 보통으로 하실래요, 등기로 하실래요?
        A: 보통으로 해 주세요.

(2)   (Buying something at the post office)
        손님: 우표 10장 주세요.
        우체국 직원: 얼마짜리 드릴까요?
        손님: 340원짜리로 주세요. 참, 엽서는 한 장에 얼마예요?
        우체국 직원: 한 장에 650원입니다.
        손님: 그럼, 세 장 주세요.
        우체국 직원: 여기 있습니다.
        손님: 전부(all) 얼마예요?
        우체국 직원: 5,350원입니다.

You may hear the following expressions from a postal clerk.

우체국 직원: 몇 장 드릴까요?/필요하세요?
                  여기 있어요.
                  (소포) 어디 보내실 거예요?
                  소포 안에 뭐 들어 있어요?

Useful words

우편 mail service, 우편 번호 a postal code, 우편 요금 postage, 엽서 a postcard, 봉투 an envelope, 주소 an address, 답장('a reply')을 쓰다/보내다, 우표를 붙이다 to put a stamp on, 소포를 찾다 to pick up a package

[Exercise 1] Practice the following conversation. (Mark wants to borrow a stamp and an envelope from his roommate Woojin.)

> 마크: 우진 씨, 미안하지만 <u>우표</u> 있으면 한 장 주실래요?
>
> 우진: 네, 있어요. 드릴게요.
>
> 마크: 참, <u>봉투</u>도 있으면 한 장 주세요.
>
> 우진: <u>봉투</u>는 없는데요.

Practice the above conversation again, substituting the following for the underlined parts.

> (1)   엽서   (2)   편지 봉투

[Exercise 2] Practice the following dialogue.

> 마크: 민지 씨, 어디 가세요?
>
> 민지: <u>우표 사러</u> 우체국에 가는 길이에요.
>
> 마크: 잘 됐네요. 그럼 우체국에서 이 편지 좀 부쳐 주실래요?
>
> 민지: 네, 그러죠.
>
> 마크: 고맙습니다.
>
> 민지: 뭘요. 가는 길인데요.

Take the roles of 마크 and 민지. Change the underlined parts above with the following expressions and practice the conversation again.

> (1)   소포(를) 부치다
>
> (2)   엽서(를) 사다
>
> (3)   생일 카드(를) 보내다
>
> (4)   소포(를) 찾다

[Exercise 3] You are in Seoul and want to mail a postcard (엽서) to your friend at Jeju University. You need to find out the postage and the postal code (우편 번호). Complete the following dialogue between a postal clerk and you.

You:　이 엽서 제주도에 보내려고 하는데요.

_____?

직원:　340원짜리 두 장 붙이시면 돼요.

You:　_____?

직원:　이삼 일 정도 걸립니다.

You:　_____?

직원:　잠깐만 기다려 보세요.

제주 대학 우편 번호는 690-756입니다.

[Exercise 4] (Role-play) Take the roles of a postal clerk and a customer for the following situations:

(1)　A customer wants to buy ten 250-won stamps.

(2)　A customer wants to buy five envelopes.

(3)　A customer wants to mail a package containing a book to Sydney.

2. Giving a warning and seeking advice

Examples

(1)　직원:　손님, 포장(packing)을 이렇게 하시면 안 돼요.

손님:　그럼, 어떻게 해야 돼요?

직원:　상자에 담아서 테이프(tape)로 잘 붙이셔야죠.

손님:　네, 알겠습니다.

(2)　선생님:수업 시간에 영어를 쓰면 안 돼요.

학생:　그럼 모르는 게 있으면 어떻게 해야 돼요?

선생님:수업이 끝나고 영어로 물어 보세요.

학생:　네, 알겠습니다.

(3)   A: 주말에 소포를 보내려면 어느 우체국에 가야 돼요?

       B: 중앙 우체국에 가셔야지요.

       A: 중앙 우체국에 가려면 몇 번 버스를 타야 돼요?

       B: 480번을 타세요.

       A: 미국에 엽서를 보내려면 얼마짜리 우표를 붙여야 돼요?

       B: 400원짜리(worth)를 붙이세요.

When giving advice or a warning, the negative conditional form ~(으)면 안 되다 'You shouldn't . . ., Please don't . . .'(Lit., 'If you do . . ., it is not good.') is often used, as illustrated below.

수업 시간에 영어를   A Korean language teacher tells students
쓰면 안 됩니다.   not to use English during class.

손님, 포장을 이렇게   A postal clerk gives a customer advice
하시면 안 됩니다.   on wrapping packages.

For seeking advice, you can say 그럼, 어떻게 해야 돼요? 'Then, what should I do?/What am I supposed to do?'. To express an opinion or to give advice, ~어/아야지요 'should, ought to' is often used. For example, at a post office, a customer is about to leave without taking his/her change.

Clerk: 손님, 거스름돈 받아 가셔야지요.
Customer: 아, 네. 고맙습니다.

[Exercise 1] Give your opinion or advice for the following situations.

       (1)   한국어를 잘하고 싶어요.

       (2)   아르바이트를 하고 싶은데 어떻게 찾아요?

       (3)   숙제를 하기 싫을 때는 어떻게 해야 돼요?

              (~기 싫다 'to hate to do . . .')

       (4)   몸이 아플 때 어떻게 해요?

       (5)   싼 비행기 표를 사고 싶은데 어떻게 하는 게 좋을까요?

       (6)   좋은 친구를 사귀고 싶어요.

3. Writing personal letters

Read the following letter and answer the questions.

그리운 어머니께,

　　그동안 안녕하셨어요? 할머니, 아버지께서도 안녕하시지요? 저도 몸 건강히 잘 지내고 있습니다. 먼저 어머니의 생신을 축하 드립니다. 여기 작은 선물을 보냅니다. 어머니께서 좋아하시는 빨간 색 옷을 샀습니다. 어머니 마음에 드셨으면 좋겠어요.
　　이 곳은 이제 또 새 학기가 시작되어 바빠지기 시작했습니다. 어서 이번 학기를 끝내고 미국으로 돌아가고 싶습니다. 식구들도 보고 싶고, 어머니께서 만드신 맛있는 음식도 먹고 싶습니다. 누나하고 형한테도 제 안부 전혜 주세요. 그럼 또 편지 쓰겠습니다. 안녕히 계세요.

　　　　　　　　　　　　　　　　　　　2015년 8월 30일
　　　　　　　　　　　　　　　　　　　　　서울에서
　　　　　　　　　　　　　　　　　　　　우진 올림

[Exercise 1] Reading comprehension

　　(1)　What present did Woojin buy for his mother?
　　(2)　List all of Woojin's family members.
　　(3)　How did Woojin describe his recent life in Korea?
　　(4)　What did Woojin wish to do?

[Exercise 2] Imagine that you are sending a birthday present to your friend in Korea. Write a letter to her/him.

Lesson 4. Life in Korea I

CONVERSATION 1: I am on my way to Insadong.

(By chance, Minji met Woojin at the dormitory's entrance.)

Minji:	Woojin, where are you going?
Woojin:	I am on my way to Insadong to buy a present.
Minji:	Why?
Woojin:	Because my mom's birthday is at the end of this month.
Minji:	Oh, is that so? What are you going to buy?
Woojin:	I am thinking of buying a set of spoons and chopsticks.
Minji:	That is a good idea. If you go to Insadong, you will be able to buy something you like because it has many Korean traditional crafts shops.
Woojin:	If you happen to have time now, will you go together with me?
Minji:	Okay, I will, but I have to withdraw money from the bank on our way there.
Woojin:	Okay, you can do that.

CONVERSATION 2: I would like to send a package.

(Woojin went to the post office in order to send a package to the United States.)

Clerk:	Welcome. How can I help you?
Woojin:	How long does it take if I send a package to the United States?
Clerk:	Where in the United States?
Woojin:	New York.
Clerk:	It takes about three days.
Woojin:	Is that so? It sounds good.
Clerk:	What is inside the package? Is it fragile?
Woojin:	It is not. It is a set of spoons and chopsticks.
Clerk:	(Giving him a paper) If you want to send a package, please write the address here.
Woojin:	Okay, here it is. Thank you for your help. (Woojin leaves.)
Clerk:	Excuse me, hold on. You should take the receipt.
Woojin:	Oh, yes. Thank you.

NARRATION: Woojin's letter

Dear Mom whom I miss,

How have you been so far? I am doing well and am in good health. First of all, happy birthday, Mom. I bought you a pretty set of spoons and chopsticks from Korea. I hope you will like them.

You must have worried about me a lot, since I didn't answer the phone the last time you called me. At that time, I was studying at the library all day long. It turned out that I will receive a scholarship because my grades were very good this semester. You don't have to send me tuition. I have gotten used to school life and have made many friends. So please don't worry about me. And please always be healthy. I miss all my family. I will write you again soon. Goodbye.

June 30, 2013
From Woojin in Seoul

CULTURE: Insadong

If you want to taste Korean traditional culture and food, you have to go to Insadong without fail. Insadong is a street reaching from Anguk Station to Jongno 2-ga in Seoul. You can take the subway line 3 and get off at Anguk Station and walk to Insadong.

There are many antique and crafts stores and also many galleries, traditional teahouses, and traditional restaurants as well. Walking on the Insadong street, you can see students examining the craft items, foreigners buying merchandise, college students who date at the teahouse, and old men and women who eat Korean traditional food at the Korean restaurants. In other words, Insadong is a place where people of all sorts—such as young students and old men and ladies and foreigners as well—often go because there are many things to see and eat. Insadong, the center of Korean traditional culture, is a place definitely worth visiting in Seoul.

5과 한국 생활 II [Life in Korea II]

| Conversation 1 | 방값도 싸고 괜찮아. |

우진: 수빈아, 잘 지냈어?G5.1

수빈: 응, 잘 지냈어.

우진: 혹시 좋은 원룸 알면 소개 좀 해 줄래?

수빈: 왜? 이사하려고?

우진: 응, 요새 원룸으로 옮길까 해.

수빈: 지금 사는 아파트가 불편해?

우진: 아니. 교통도 편하고 집주인도 친절한데
방 값이 좀 비싼 편이라서.G5.2
학교 앞 원룸들 어때?

수빈: 내 친구 하나가 학교 앞
원룸에 사는데
방 값도 싸고
괜찮은 것 같아.

우진: 아, 그럼, 학교 앞 원룸을
알아봐야겠네.
그런데, 수빈아, 가구를 사려는데 어디가
제일 좋은지 알아? G5.3

수빈: 글쎄, 잘 모르겠는데. 친구한테 한번 물어볼게.

COMPREHENSION QUESTIONS

1. 우진이는 왜 이사하려고 합니까?
2. 우진이는 어떤 방을 찾고 있습니까?
3. 우진이는 무엇을 사고 싶어합니까?

NEW WORDS

NOUN		VERB	
가구	furniture	구하다	to search for
가구점	furniture store	벗다	to take off
거실	living room	옮기다	to move, shift
배달	delivery	지나가다	to pass by
사무실	office	**ADJECTIVE**	
소개(하다)	introduction	부족하다	to be insufficient
아주머니	middle-aged woman	진절하다	to be kind
옷장	wardrobe, closet	**ADVERB**	
원룸	studio apartment	반드시	surely, certainly
주인	owner	요새	these days
책장	bookshelf, bookcase	**SUFFIX**	
침대	bed	~(으)ㄴ/는 편이다	to tend to
침실	bedroom	~(으)ㄴ/는지	to know/not know
통화(하다)	phone call	알다/모르다	whether
하숙방	a room in a	~어/아	intimate speech style
	boardinghouse	아/야	vocative suffix
하숙비	boarding expenses	**INTERJECTION**	
하숙집	boardinghouse	응	yeah
PRONOUN			
너	you (plain form)		

NEW EXPRESSIONS

1. In 수빈아, the plain-level vocative particle 아 is attached at the end of someone's first name to draw the attention of the addressee in a discourse context. The particle 아 is attached after a name that ends with a consonant (e.g., 수빈아); after a name that ends with a vowel, the particle 야 is used instead (e.g., 민지야).

These particles are typically used to address a child by another child or an adult; they are also used to address an adult by his or her parents or by a friend whose friendship began in childhood.

2. 혹시 'by any chance, in case, possibly' is used often in a conditional sentence or in a question.

3. 옮기다 and 이사하다 are used interchangeably in the text but, there are some differences between the two. 이사하다 means basically 'to move one's residence' while 옮기다 has the wider range of meanings 'to move (things), transfer, translate' and 'to infect (with disease)'.

4. 사려는데 is a contracted form of 사려고 하는데. 고 하 is omitted in other constructions as in 사려면 (from 사려고 하면 'if you want to buy').

GRAMMAR

G5.1   The intimate speech style ~어/아

Examples

(1)   마크: 여보세요.
       동수: 마크, 나**야**.   Mark, it's me. Did you call
              아까 전화했**어**?   me a little while ago?
       마크: 응, 혹시 내일 등산 **갈 거야**?
       동수: 응, 왜? 너도 같이 갈**래**?

(2)   마크: 응. 그럼, 내일 아침에 전화할**까**?
       동수: 그러지 말고, 그냥 아침에 우리 집으로 **와**.
       마크: 응, 알았**어**.

(3)   A: 지금 사는 하숙집 어**때**?
       B: 하숙비도 싸고 가구가 있어서 편**해**.
             침대랑 옷장도 있고 책장도 두 개나 있**어**.

Notes

1. Between close people, e.g., friends from childhood, siblings, etc., the so-

called intimate (speech) style is used. The intimate style is represented by the ending ~어/아.

2. Note that the polite style ~어요/아요 consists of the intimate style ending ~어/아 followed by the polite marker ~요. Therefore, the intimate style is subject to the same variation as the polite ~어요/아요 style. That is, the form is ~아 if the last vowel of the verb stem is either 아 or 오, as in 좋아, except that the ending ~아 is deleted if the stem ends in 아 or 애 without a final consonant, as in 가. Otherwise the form is ~어, as in 있어. When the predicate is -하다, 하+어 renders 해, as in 편해 in (3) (cf. 편해요). After the past-tense marker ~었/았, ~어 is used regardless of the stem vowel.

Note also the following variations.

After the copula 이, ~야 is attached, as in 나야 in (1):

| 저예요 | → | 나야 |
| 갈 거예요 | → | 갈 거야 |

When the stem ends in 오, as in 오다, the stem and the intimate ending are contracted to 와, as in (2):

오+아 → 와

For other endings, the intimate style is made by deleting the polite marker ~요 from the polite style, as in 어때 in (3): cf. 어때요.

	Dictionary form	Polite style	Intimate style	~었/았-	~(으)ㄹ래
~아	이다	이에요/예요	(이)야	이었어/였어	*
	좋다	좋아요	좋아	좋았어	*
	작다	작아요	작아	작았어	*
	찾다	찾아요	찾아	찾았어	찾을래
	가다	가요	가	갔어	갈래

~어	있다	있어요	있어	있었어	있을래
	쉬다	쉬어요	쉬어	쉬었어	쉴래
C o n t r a c t e d	보다	봐요	봐	봤어	볼래
	오다	와요	와	왔어	올래
	어렵다	어려워요	어려워	어려웠어	*
	쉽다	쉬워요	쉬워	쉬웠어	*
	전화하다	전화해요	전화해	전화했어	전화할래
	되다	돼요	돼	됐어	될래

[* indicates that the form is not available because of the semantic nature of the predicate. Adjectives cannot be used with the intention suffix ~(으)ㄹ래 because intention requires an action.]

3. When the intimate speech style is used, expressions such as 'yes' and 'no' must be switched to non-polite forms as in (1) and (2):

네/예   →   응

아니요   →   아니

Exercise

Convert the given dialogue into the intimate speech style.

(1)   A: 어디까지 가세요?   →   어디까지 가?

      B: 관악역까지 가요.   →   관악역까지 가.

(2)   A: 가게 주인 아주머니는 어디 가셨어요?

      B: 물건 배달 가셨는데요. 왜요?

(3)   A: 왜 요즘 그렇게 연락을 안 했어요?

      B: 미안해요. 좀 바빴거든요.

(4)   A: 저 사람은 누구예요?

      B: 아마 린다 동생일 거예요.

(5)   A: 하숙방은 구하셨어요?

      B: 아니요, 아직 알아보고 있어요.

| G5.2 | ~(으)ㄴ/는 편이다 'it is more the case of . . . than the other' |

Examples

(1) A: 새로 이사간 아파트 어때?
    B: 침실은 작지만 거실이 넓**은 편이야**.

(2) A: 요즘 부모님 건강이 어떠세요?
    B: 건강하**신 편이에요**.   They are on the healthy side.

(3) A: 보통 몇 시에 주무세요?
    B: 늦게 자**는 편이에요**.

(4) A: 서울 물가가 어때요?
    B: 도쿄(Tokyo)보다는 싸지만 비**싼 편이에요**.

Notes

1. 편 literally means 'a side, a group, a team', as in
      우리 편 'our team'   상대편 'the opponent'
      이 편 'this side'   저 편 'that side' or 'the other side'

2. ~(으)ㄴ/는 편이다, literally meaning 'It belongs to the side of . . .', is an expression of approximation that gives the effect of saying 'I cannot say this or that, but if you ask me to choose one way or the other, I would say it is more this way than the other.'

3. As noun-modifying forms, ~(으)ㄴ 편이다 is used for adjectives and ~는 편이다 for verbs.

Exercise

Using ~(으)ㄴ/는 편이에요, answer the following questions.

   (1)   A: 골프 자주 치세요?
         B: 네, 일주일에 두 번 치니까 <u>자주 치는 편이에요</u>.

(2)   소연: 새로 이사 간 동네 어때?

성희: 응, 좋아. 슈퍼마켓도 가깝고 교통도 _____

(3)   성희: 스티브 씨, 영화 보는 거 좋아해요?

스티브:_____

특히 코미디를 좋아해요.

(4)   A: 음악회 자주 가세요?

B: 네, 요즘은 잘 못 가지만 _____

한 달에 한 번 정도 가요.

(5)   소연: 성희야, 왜 백화점에 안 가고 여기 왔어?

성희: 여기가 백화점보다 _____

(6)   성희: 소연아, 하루에 몇 시간 자?

소연: _____

하루에 5시간밖에 못 자서 항상 잠이 부족해.

G5.3	~(으)ㄴ/는지 알다/모르다 'know/don't know whether (what, who, where, when) . . .'

Examples

Verb~는지:

(1)	우진: 민지 씨, 우체국이 어디 있**는지 아세요?** 민지: 네, 알아요.	Minji, do you know where the post office is?

(2)   한국에서는 방에서 반드시
신발을 벗어야 되**는지 몰랐어요**.

Adj.~(으)ㄴ지:

(3)   A: 가구를 사려고 하는데
어디가 제일 싼**지 아세요?**

B: 은행 앞에 있는 가구점이
제일 싸요.

N~(이)ㄴ지:

(4) A: 오늘이 무슨 날**인지 아세요?**

　　B: 아니요, 무슨 날인데요?

　　A: 제 생일이에요.

~었는지/았는지:

(5) 우진: 샌디 씨, 작년에 한국어를　　　　　Sandy, do you know
　　　　　누가 가르쳤**는지 아세요?**　　　who taught Korean
　　　　　　　　　　　　　　　　　　　last year?

　　샌디: 네, 이 선생님께서 가르치셨어요.

(6) A: 어제가 무슨 날이었**는지 아세요?**

　　B: 한글날(Hangul Day)이요.

(7) A: 스티브가 어디에 갔**는지 모르겠어요.**

　　B: 조금 전에 지나갔는데 못 봤어요?

Notes

1. ~(으)ㄴ/는지 introduces an indirect question. It occurs with question words such as 어디 (where), 무엇 (what), 무슨 (which . . ., what kind of . . .), 누구/누가 (who), 어떻게 (how), 얼마나 (how much/many), 언제 (when), 왜 (why), etc., and is followed by either 알다 or 모르다.

2. In the non-past tense, it shows the same variation in conjugation of predicate as noun-modifying forms; that is, verbs take ~는지, whereas adjectives and the copula -이 take ~(으)ㄴ지 and ~(이)ㄴ지, respectively.

In the past tense, on the other hand, it is ~었는지/았는지 regardless of predicate types.

	~(으)ㄴ/는지		Noun-modifying forms	
	Non-past	Past	Non-past	Past
Verb	~는지	~었는지	~는	~(으)ㄴ/던
Adjective	~(으)ㄴ지	~었/았는지	~(으)ㄴ	~던
Copula	~(이)ㄴ지	~이었는지	~(이)ㄴ	~(이)던

Exercises

1. Fill in the blanks using the appropriate forms of ~(으)ㄴ/는지.

      (1)   민지가 왜 기분이 (좋다)_____ 알아?

                지금 남자 친구랑 통화하고 있거든.

      (2)   김 교수님 어디 (계시다) _____알아요?

                아마 사무실에 계실 거예요.

      (3)   기숙사가 왜 이렇게 (조용하다)_____ 아세요?

                학생들이 모두 집으로 돌아갔거든요.

      (4)   상자에 뭐가 (들어있다) _____ 알아요?

                지난 학기에 쓰던 책이요.

2. Ask your classmates the following questions using the ~는지/(으)ㄴ지 아세요? 'Do you know . . .?'

      (1)   Who invented the Korean alphabet (Hangeul)?

      (2)   When is Hangeul Day?

      (3)   How many days are there in May?

      (4)   Where is the closest post office?

      (5)   When is the final exam for Korean class this term?

      (6)   What language do they speak in Chile?

      (7)   Who is the richest man in America?

      (8)   Why did John not come to school yesterday?

(Variation) Go around the classroom and find the person who knows the answer.

Conversation 2 | 이사 온 지 얼마나 됐어요?

(스티브가 새로 이사 온 하숙집에서 에이미와 이야기합니다.)

스티브: 안녕하세요. 새로 이사 온 스티브예요.

에이미: 아, 네. 안녕하세요. 저는 에이미예요.
이사 온 지 얼마나 됐어요?[G5.4]

스티브: 어제 이사 왔어요.

에이미: 그럼 짐 정리도 아직 안 됐겠네요.

스티브: 대충 됐는데 인터넷 연결이 잘 안 되네요.

에이미: 아, 그래요? 그럼 피시방에 가 보세요.
돈을 내고 인터넷을 사용할 수 있어요.

스티브: 아, 그런 곳이 있어요?

에이미: 네, 한국에는 가게들 이름이 무슨무슨 방이
많아요. 피시방, 노래방, 만화방, 그리고
찜질방도 있어요.

스티브: 찜질방은 뭐
하는 데예요?

에이미: 목욕도 하고
사우나도 하고
쉬기도 하는
곳이에요.

스티브: 신기하네요.

에이미: 공부하다가[G5.5] 힘들면 한번 가 보세요.
스트레스도 풀 수 있어 좋아요.

COMPREHENSION QUESTIONS

1. 스티브는 하숙집으로 언제 이사 왔습니까?
2. 피시방은 어떤 곳입니까?
3. 찜질방은 어떤 곳입니까?

NEW WORDS

NOUN		VERB	
냉장고	refrigerator	넘어지다	to fall (down)
만화방	comic book rental	눕다	to lie down
	store	돌아가다	to return (to)
바닥	floor	사 먹다	to buy and eat
사우나	sauna	사귀다	② to date
사투리	dialect	잠이 들다	to fall asleep
세탁기	washing machine	헤어지다	to break up
소파	sofa	**ADJECTIVE**	
식탁	dining table	그립다	to miss, long for
아르바이트	part-time job	신기하다	to be amazing
연결(하다)	connection, link	안전하다	to be safe
운전 면허	driver's license	**ADVERB**	
정리(하다)	arrangement	대충	roughly
지갑	wallet	방금	a moment ago
지방	region, district	**SUFFIX**	
찜질방	Korean dry sauna	~(으)ㄴ/는 지	It has been [time span]
청소기	vacuum cleaner	[ ] 되다	since . . .
피시방	Internet café	~다가	movement from one
			action/state to another

NEW EXPRESSIONS

1. 되 vs. 돼
Because the pronunciations are almost identical, this is a source for misspelling for both native speakers and foreign learners. 되 is a stem form, while 돼 is a combination of 되 + ~어 as shown below.

됩니다	돼요 (= 되어요)	되면
돼서 (= 되어서)	되는	됐어요 (= 되었어요)
되지만	됐는데 (= 되었는데)	

2. In 무슨무슨 방, speakers duplicate the indefinite pronoun 무슨 'something, some kind of' to be used as an expression like "such and such".

3. In 있어 좋아요, the suffix 서 is omitted from 있어서 좋아요.

GRAMMAR

G5.4	A: ~(으)ㄴ 지 얼마나 됐어요? 'How long has it been since . . . ?' B: ~(으)ㄴ 지 TIME SPAN(이/가) 됐어요. 'It has been . . . since . . .'

Examples

(1) 소연: 한국에 오**신 지 얼마나 됐어요?** How long has it been since you came to Korea?

마크: (한국에 **온 지**) 이제 **반 년 됐는데** 벌써 친구들이 그리워요. Now it's been half a year (since I came to Korea), and I already miss my friends.

(2) A: 운전면허 받**은 지 얼마나 됐어요?**
B: 1년 됐어요.

(3) A: 점심 먹으러 갈래요?
B: 벌써요? 아침 먹**은 지 2시간밖에 안 됐어요.**

(4) A: 백화점에서 뭐 사셨어요?
B: 냉장고하고 청소기요.
이사온 **지 하루밖에 안 돼서** 필요한 게 많거든요.

(5) 동수는 지방에서 서울로 **온 지** 벌써 2년이나 됐는데 아직도 사투리를 써요.

Notes

1. TIME SPAN(이/가) 되다 indicates the amount of time that has passed since a certain time.

2. ~(으)ㄴ 지 TIME SPAN(이/가) 되다 expresses the amount of time that has elapsed since the event at issue took place. The reference event is expressed in ~(으)ㄴ 지. It can best be translated as 'It has been [TIME SPAN] since . . .' or '[TIME SPAN] has passed since . . .' The question asking about the time lapse is made with the question word 얼마나, hence ~(으)ㄴ 지 얼마나 됐어요? 'How long has it been since . . .?'

3. TIME SPAN이/가 되다 is typically in the past tense form.

Exercise

Make up dialogues based on the given information, following the pattern as in (1).

(1)   [민지는 3년 전에 피아노를 배우기 시작했습니다.]

　　　린다:　민지 씨, 피아노 배운 지 얼마나 됐어요?

　　　민지:　3년 됐어요.

(2)   [스티브는 6개월 전에 미국으로 돌아갔습니다.]

　　　민지: _____

　　　스티브:_____

(3)   [동수는 지난 주에 새 지갑을 선물 받았습니다.]

　　　소연: _____

　　　동수: _____

(4)   [샌디는 1년 전에 아르바이트를 시작했습니다.]

　　　성희: _____

　　　샌디: _____

(5)   [성희는 4달 전에 하숙집에서 살기 시작했습니다.]

　　　소연: _____

　　　성희: _____

(6)   [소연이는 3일 전에 새 냉장고하고 세탁기를 샀습니다.]

　　　성희: _____

　　　소연: _____

| G5.5 | ~다가: transference of an action/state to another |

Examples

(1) 스티브는 그동안 아파트에서 살**다가** 학교 앞 하숙집으로 옮겼습니다. During that time, Steve had lived in an apartment and then moved to a 하숙집 that is in front of his school.

(2) 동수는 수잔이랑 사귀**다가** 작년에 헤어졌어요. Dongsoo and Susan had been dating but then broke up last year.

(3) 마크는 학교에서 나오**다가** 샌디를 만났어요. On his way coming out of school, Mark met Sandy.

(4) 린다가 소파에 누워 있**다가** 방금 잠이 들었어요. While lying down on a sofa, Linda fell asleep a moment ago.

Notes

1. The suffix ~다가 indicates that momentum is transferred from one action or state to another; that is, a person or an object engaged in an action or a state of affairs turns to another action or state.

2. ~다가 indicates a shift, but one that takes place only after the earlier action has been completed as in (1) and (2). It may be translated as '. . . was (engaged in) ~ing, then . . .'

3. ~다가 is also used to indicate that a new action or state occurs in the middle of the first action or state; that is, the first action has not reached its endpoint as in (3) and (4). It may be variously translated as 'in the middle of ~ing', 'while ~ing', 'on the way to . . .'

Exercises

1. Describe what happened while you were engaged in the given action.

(1) On my way home: 집에 오다가 스티브를 만났어요.

(2)   On the way to school: _____

(3)   While playing basketball: _____

(4)   I was dozing off during the class: _____

(5)   I was going shopping: _____

2. Say in Korean what you would do when the situation specified in parentheses occurs while you are engaged in the given situation.

(1)   I am studying. (피곤해지다)

       공부하다가 피곤해지면 나가서 운동을 해요.

(2)   I am on my way back home. (배가 고프다)

       _____

(3)   I am sleeping. (목이 마르다)

       _____

(4)   I am driving. (졸리다)

       _____

(5)   I am eating. (배가 아프다)

       _____

3. Describe how your earlier action has changed.

(1)   한국에서 공부하다가 지난 달에 미국으로 돌아왔어요.

(2)   2년 동안 일하다가 _____

(3)   여름 방학에 쉬다가 _____

(4)   매일 햄버거만 먹다가 _____

(5)   두 학기 동안 한국어를 배우다가 _____

(6)   룸메이트하고 같이 살다가 _____

(7)   항상 콜라만 마시다가 _____

Narration 스티브의 하숙방

스티브가 한국에 온 지도 벌써 6개월이 됐습니다.
스티브는 그동안 학교 기숙사에서 살다가 지난 주말에
학교 앞 하숙집으로 옮겼습니다. 하숙집은 방은 작지만
주인 아주머니가 아주 친절하시고 하숙비도 싼 편입니다.
또한, 하숙집은 아침과 저녁을 주기 때문에 점심만
학교에서 사 먹으면 됩니다.

스티브의 하숙방은 온돌방입니다. 침대는 없고, 책상과
책장, 그리고 작은 옷장이 있습니다. 온돌방은 바닥이
따뜻해서 추운 겨울에도 바닥에서 잘 수 있습니다.
스티브는 처음에는 온돌방이 불편했지만, 이제는 미국에
돌아가면 온돌방이 그리울 것 같습니다.

온돌 'floor heating system'

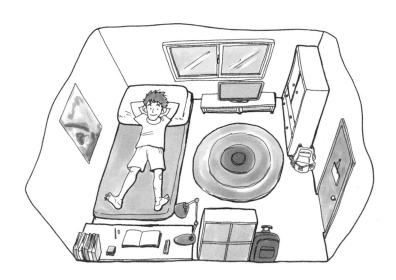

COMPREHENSION QUESTIONS

1. 스티브는 하숙집으로 이사오기 전에 어디서 살았습니까?
2. 새로 이사온 하숙집은 어떻습니까?
3. 스티브 방 안에는 어떤 가구가 있습니까?
4. 온돌방은 무엇이 좋습니까?

NEW EXPRESSION

아주머니, a kinship term for 'aunt', is used here to refer to a middle-aged woman.

CULTURE

하숙과 자취

한국의 대학생들은 보통 부모님과 같이 삽니다. 그런데 집하고 학교가 먼 경우에는 학교 근처에서 하숙이나 자취를 하기도 합니다. 하숙은 집 주인에게 방값과 식비를 내고 주인 집에서 먹고 자는 경우를 말합니다. 주인 아주머니가 보통 아침과 저녁 식사를 준비해 줍니다. 하숙집에서 다른 하숙생들과 생활하기 때문에 친구들도 많이 사귈 수 있고 외롭지 않아서 좋습니다.

하숙 생활이 불편한 학생들은 자취를 합니다. 자취는 직접 밥도 하고 빨래와 청소를 하면서 사는 경우입니다. 주인 집에서 방만 빌리는 경우도 있고 오피스텔이나 원룸과 같은 곳을 빌리는 경우도 있습니다. 한국의 '원룸'은 미국의 studio를 말합니다. 오피스텔은 오피스와 호텔을 줄인 말입니다. 낮에는 일을 하거나 공부를 하고 밤에는 잠을 자는 곳입니다. 원룸이나 오피스텔 생활이 편리하기 때문에 요즘은 직장인들도 원룸과 오피스텔에서 많이 삽니다.

경우	case	자취(하다)	to live on one's own
식비	food expenses	줄이다	to shorten
외롭다	to be lonely	직장인	office worker

USAGE

1. Searching for housing

Examples

(1) 성희: 마크 씨, 지금 어디 사세요?
 마크: 학교 근저 아파트에 살고 있어요.
 성희: 그래요? 아파트가 좋아요?
 마크: 괜찮아요. 동네도 조용하고 교통도 편리하고 건물도 깨끗해요. 성희 씨 지금 살고 있는 아파트는 어때요?
 성희: 방도 넓고 다 좋은데, 방 값이 좀 비싸요.
 마크: 얼마예요?
 성희: 한 달에 800불이에요.

(2) A: 요즘 방 보러 다니는 중이에요.
 B: 어떤 방을 구하세요(looking for)?
 A: 교통이 편리하고 방이 넓고 깨끗했으면 좋겠어요.
 B: 신문 광고(advertisement) 보셨어요?
 A: 네, 그런데 아직 좋은 걸 못 찾았어요.

[Exercise 1] Converse with your partner about the following questions.

(1) 지금 어디 사세요? (아파트, 기숙사, 하숙집, etc.)

(2) 한 달에 방값이 얼마예요?

(3) 언제 방값을 내야 돼요?

(4) 빨래는 보통 어디서 해요?

(5) 교통이 편리해요?

[Exercise 2] Take different roles to practice the following conversation.

A: 요즘 아파트 보러 다니는 중이에요.

B: 어떤 방을 찾으세요?

A: <u>교통이 편리하고 방이 넓고 깨끗했으면 좋겠어요.</u>

B: 신문 광고 보셨어요?

A: 네. 그런데 좋은 아파트는 너무 비싸요.

Substitute the underlined part above with the following:

(1)   You want to rent a quiet studio near your school.

(2)   You want to rent an apartment in a safe neighborhood.

(3)   You want to rent a room with a private bathroom in a nice house.

[Exercise 3] Draw a line from each question to an appropriate answer between a prospective tenant and a landlord. Then practice with your partner.

독방 'a single room'

실례합니다. 주인 계십니까? •   • 마침 방이 하나 있어요.

독방 있어요?   •   • 전데요. 어떻게 오셨어요?

하숙비는 어떻게 돼요?   •   • 방 옆에 있어요.

이번 주말에 이사해도 돼요? •   • 한 달에 삼십만 원이에요.

화장실은 어디 있어요?   •   • 화장실에 세탁기가 있어요.

빨래는 어디서 해요?   •   • 네, 그럼요.

2. Describing buildings and interiors

Examples

소연: 어머, 이 책상 참 좋네요. 어디서 사셨어요?

스티브: 신문 광고 보고 샀어요. 중고품이에요.

소연: 꼭 새 거 같이 보이는데, 이게 중고 가구예요?
스티브: 네, 저도 중고 가구점에 가서 보고 놀랐어요.
소연: 싸게 샀겠네요. 얼마 주셨어요?
스티브: 20불 줬어요.
소연: 와, 정말 싸네요.

(중고품 'used merchandise', 중고 가구 'used furniture', 놀라다 'to be surprised')

[Exercise 1] Practice the conversation above again, substituting the following for 책상.

      (1)   텔레비전
      (2)   책장
      (3)   식탁
      (4)   소파
      (5)   냉장고

[Exercise 2] Read the following letter that Steve wrote to his teacher in New York and answer the questions.

이민수 선생님께,
      선생님, 그동안 안녕하셨습니까?
제가 한국에 온 지도 벌써 반년이 됐습니다. 저는 그동안 학교 근처
아파트에 살다가 지난 주 토요일에 하숙집으로 이사했습니다. 아파트에
살 때는 매일 밥을 해 먹는 게 힘들었는데, 새로 이사한 하숙집에서는
아침, 저녁 식사를 다 주니까 참 편리합니다. 하숙집 음식도 맛있고
주인 아주머니도 아주 친절합니다. 미국에 다시 돌아갈 때까지 계속 이
하숙집에서 살려고 합니다. 좋은 방을 찾기도 힘들고, 또 이사를 하기도
쉽지 않기 때문입니다.
      제가 지금 살고 있는 하숙집은 온돌방입니다. 방안에는 책상, 옷장,
컴퓨터, 책장이 두 개 있습니다. 하숙집은 학교까지 걸어서 20분 정도
걸립니다. 이 곳에 사는 하숙생들은 거의 다 저하고 같은 학교에 다니는

대학생들입니다. 중국에서 온 남학생도 한 명 있습니다. 하숙집 앞에는 작은 슈퍼도 있고 또 찜질방이 있어서 참 편리합니다.

그럼 또 연락 드리겠습니다. 거기 한국어 반 친구들한테 안부 전해 주십시오.

2013년 9월 12일
서울에서
스티브 올림

Mark T(rue) or F(alse) for the following statements.

(1)   _____ Steve came to Korea a year ago.

(2)   _____ Steve used to live in a dormitory in Seoul.

(3)   _____ The boardinghouse does not offer lunch.

(4)   _____ Steve plans to stay in the same house until graduation.

(5)   _____ Steve does not have a bed in his room.

(6)   _____ It takes only ten minutes from Steve's place to school.

Useful words

안방 the master bedroom, 화장실 a bathroom, 부엌 a kitchen, 거실 a living room, 공부방 a study room, 현관 the entrance, 차고 a garage, 마당/정원 a yard, 이층 the second floor, 일층 the first floor, 아래층 the downstairs, 수영장 a swimming pool

가구 furniture, 침대 a bed, 책상 a desk, 의자 a chair, 사진 a photo, 세탁기 a washer, 옷장/장롱 a closet, 서랍 a drawer, 냉장고 a refrigerator, 소파 a sofa, 램프 a lamp, 그릇 a dish, 식탁 a dining table, 청소기 a vacuum cleaner

[Exercise 3] Write a letter to one of your friends describing the apartment (including furniture) or house you live in.

3. Initiating a conversation and introducing oneself

Examples

(1) 소연: 혹시 스티브 씨 아니세요?
     스티브: 네, 그런데요.
     소연: 저 성희 친구 최소연이에요. 성희한테서 스티브 씨
               말씀 많이 들었어요.
     스티브: 아, 최소연 씨세요? 저도 말씀 많이 들었습니다.
               앞으로 잘 부탁 드립니다.
     소연: 저도요. 반갑습니다. 여기 이사하신 지 얼마나
               됐어요?
     스티브: 일주일 됐어요.

(2) 영미: 저어, 실례지만 혹시 김철수 씨 아니세요?
     철수: 네, 그런데요. 저를 어떻게 아세요?
     영미: 나 모르겠어? 고등학교 때 같은 학교에 다녔잖아.
     철수: 아, 김영미!
     영미: 응! 정말 오래간만이야.

To check and confirm information, you can initiate conversation with the
structure, 혹시 . . . 아니세요/아니에요? as shown above.

When you run into an acquaintance unexpectedly, you can express your
surprise by saying the following

        아니, 영미 씨 아니세요?
        여기 웬일이세요?

[Exercise 1] (Role-play) Twenty years after you graduated from a high
school, you run across your classmate at a supermarket.

[Exercise 2] Imagine that you run into your classmate from Korean classes
ten years later on a subway in New York City. How would you start a
conversation? Make a dialogue with your classmate. Include questions
such as "How long have you been in New York?"

4. Giving compliments and responding to compliments

Examples

In Korean culture, it is usual for people to deny or respond in a negative way when they receive compliments from others. For example,

(1)   Responding when someone praises your Korean skill

      A: 한국어 배운 지 얼마나 됐어요?
      B: 이제 일 년 됐어요.
      A: 어머, 일 년밖에 안 됐는데 한국말을 참 잘 하시네요.
      B: 뭘요('Not at all.'), 아직 많이 부족해요.

(2)   Responding when someone thanks you for a present

      A: 생일 선물 감사합니다.
      B: 조그만 거예요.   'Don't mention it.' (Lit., 'It is a very small thing.')

(3)   Offering food to a guest at a party

      Host: 차린 건 없지만 많이 드세요. (Lit., 'Although I didn't prepare anything, please eat a lot.')

      Guest: 잘 먹겠습니다.

By depreciating one's Korean language skill or belittling the present or food one offers, Koreans try to express humility. The attitude of holding back or depreciating oneself is considered to be very humble (and thus polite) in Korean culture.

[Exercise 1] How would you respond to the following compliments?

      (1)   크리스마스 선물 고맙습니다.
      (2)   오늘 입은 옷 참 예쁘네요!
      (3)   그 시계 어디서 사셨어요? 아주 멋있네요.
          (멋있다 'to be stylish, attractive')

(4)   노래를 참 잘 부르시네요!

(5)   한국어를 참 잘 하세요.

(6)   구두하고 옷하고 잘 어울려요.

[Exercise 2] Practice the conversation, substituting the underlined parts with the following.

A: 골프 치신 지 얼마나 됐어요?
B: 이제 일 년 됐어요.
A: 일 년밖에 안 됐는데 참 잘 하시네요.
B: 뭘요, 아직 많이 부족해요.

(1)   피아노를 치다

(2)   스키를 타다

(3)   한국어를 배우다

(4)   테니스를 치다

(5)   볼링 치다 (bowling)

(6)   your own hobbies

Lesson 5. Life in Korea II

CONVERSATION 1: It is nice with pretty cheap rent.

Woojin:	Soobin, how are you getting along?
Soobin:	I am getting along well.
Woojin:	Will you tell me about a nice studio if you happen to know any?
Soobin:	Why? Do you want to move?
Woojin:	Yes. These days I am thinking of moving to a studio.
Soobin:	Is the apartment you are now staying at inconvenient?
Woojin:	No. It has easy access and the landlord is kind, but the rent is rather on the expensive side. How are the studios in front of the school?
Soobin:	One of my friends lives in a studio in front of the school. It seems to be nice, and the rent is pretty cheap.
Woojin:	Oh, then, I should look for a studio in front of the school. By the way, Soobin, do you know where the best place to buy furniture is?
Soobin:	I don't. I will ask my friend.

CONVERSATION 2: How long has it been since you moved here?
(Steve talks with Amy, who lives in the boardinghouse he just moved into.)

Steve:	How are you? I am Steve and just moved here.
Amy:	Oh, yes. How are you? I am Amy. How long has it been since you moved here?
Steve:	I moved here yesterday.
Amy:	Then you must have not even unpacked yet.
Steve:	I am almost done but I can't get an Internet connection.
Amy:	Is that so? Then try going to a PC room. You can pay and use the Internet.
Steve:	Oh, are there such places?
Amy:	Yes, in Korea there are many kinds of *bang* (room), such as PC room, singing room, comic book reading room, and Korean dry sauna.
Steve:	What is a Korean dry sauna for?
Amy:	It is a place where you bathe, go into a sauna, and rest.

Steve: That's amazing.
Amy: Try to go when you are tired from studying. It is nice
                because you can also release stress.

NARRATION: Steve's room for boarding

It has been six months since Steve came to Korea. Steve lived at the school dormitory at first and then moved to the boardinghouse in front of the school last weekend. The room at the boardinghouse is small, but the female owner is very kind, and the rent is on the cheap side. Also, since the boardinghouse provides breakfast and dinner, Steve has to buy and eat only lunch at school.

Steve's room has a floor heating system. There is no bed, but there is a desk, a bookshelf, and a small closet. People sleep on the floor in a room with a floor heating system because the floor is warm. At first, the room was uncomfortable for Steve, but it seems he will miss his room's floor heating system when he goes back to the United States.

CULTURE: 하숙과 자취

Korean college students usually live with their parents. But if their home is far from school, they live in a boardinghouse or live on their own near school. In a boardinghouse you pay food expenses and room rent to the house owner and eat and sleep at the owner's house. The owner usually prepares breakfast and dinner. It is good to live in a boardinghouse because you can make many friends and you don't get lonely since you live with other students.

Students for whom a boardinghouse is inconvenient do 자취. That means that you make your own food and do your own laundry and cleaning. It can mean renting one room at someone's house or renting a place such as an officetel or studio. In Korean "one room" refers to what is called a studio in America. Officetel is a combination of the words office and hotel. It is a place where you work or study during the day and sleep at night. Many office workers also live in a studio or officetel these days because it is convenient.

6과 대중교통　[Public Transportation]

| Conversation 1 | 등산 갈 준비 다 됐니? |

(동수가 스티브의 핸드폰으로 전화한다.[G6.1])

동수:　　어, 스티브. 미안해.
　　　　아까는 배터리가 없어서 전화 못 받았어.

스티브:　어, 괜찮아. 다른 게 아니고 이번 주말에
　　　　우리 관악산에 등산 가기로 했잖아.[G6.3]
　　　　그런데, 우진이가 이번 주말에 갑자기
　　　　중요한 일이 생겨서 못 갈 것 같아.

동수:　　그래? 우진이도 가면 좋은데 아쉽다.[G6.2]
　　　　할 수 없지. 너는 등산 갈 준비 다 됐니?

스티브:　응. 그런데 우리 학교 앞에서 관악산까지
　　　　바로 가는 버스가 있어?

동수: 직접 가는 버스는 없고 중간에서 갈아타야 돼.
        먼저 지하철을 타고 서울대입구역까지
        간 다음 거기서 버스로 갈아타면 돼.
스티브: 알았어. 그럼 이번 주 토요일 아침에
        관악산 입구에서 보자.

COMPREHENSION QUESTIONS

1. 스티브가 동수 집에 전화했을 때 동수는 왜 전화를 못 받았습니까?
2. 스티브는 왜 동수한테 전화했습니까?
3. 우진이는 왜 같이 못 갑니까?
4 학교 앞에서 관악산까지 어떻게 갑니까?
5. 스티브는 내일 동수를 어디서 만납니까?

NEW WORDS

NOUN		VERB	
관악산	Gwanak Mount	고장나다	to break down
남산	Nam Mount	서두르다	to hurry
대중	the public	세우다	to stop, pull over
배터리	battery	잃어버리다	to lose
서울대입구역	Seoul University Station	잡다	to catch
승차권	ride pass, ticket	지키다	to guard, protect
신호등	traffic light	**ADJECTIVE**	
약도	rough map	아쉽다	to be sorry
열쇠	key	중요하다	to be important
올해	this year	**ADVERB**	
요금	fee, fare	바로	directly
일기	journal	**COUNTER**	
자동차	automobile	개월	month
주차장	parking lot	**SUFFIX**	
중간	the middle	~기로 하다	decided to
지하도	underpass	~는/ㄴ다	plain speech style

NEW EXPRESSIONS

1. 관악산 is a mountain in the northeastern area of Seoul, next to 북한산 National Park. Seoul is surrounded by many beautiful mountains, and 도봉산 is one of the most popular among hikers.

2. 바로 means 'straight, directly, properly, immediately', or 'right away'. 직접 'directly, at first hand, personally' has an interchangeable usage with 바로 when used in the sense of 'directly'.

> 관악산까지 바로 가는 버스
> 관악산까지 직접 가는 버스

3. 버스 정류장 'a bus stop'; 기차역 'a train station'; 버스 터미널 'a bus terminal'; 택시 승차장 (= 택시 타는 곳) 'a taxi stand'.

4. 할 수 없지: the literal meaning of 할 수 없다 is 'cannot do it'. With the verb suffix ~지(요), the phrase 할 수 없지(요) is used as a fixed expression "Oh, well."

GRAMMAR

G6.1   The plain speech style ~(는/ㄴ)다

Examples

(1)   나는 보통 7시에 아침을 먹**는다**. 그리고 8시에 학교에 간**다**.

(2)   스티브가 사는 아파트는 방이 작**다**.

(3)   스티브가 새로 이사한 집은 하숙집**이다**.
         전에 살던 곳은 학교 기숙사**다**.

(4)   승차권을 잃어버려서 무료로 지하철을 **탔다**. 그래서 좀 미안**했다**.
         Since I lost the subway ticket, I got a ride without a ticket. So I felt sorry.

(5)   학교 앞 커피숍은 아주 조용하**다**. 그래서 거기서 매일 공부**한다**.

Notes

1. The plain style is mainly used in writings such as expository writings, newspaper articles, journals, academic writings, etc.
Unlike the polite ~어요/아요 style and the deferential ~습니다 style, the plain ~(는/ㄴ)다 style does not convey politeness to the listener(s) because it is not addressed to any specific listener or reader.

2. Unlike the polite ~어요/아요 and the deferential ~습니다 styles, the plain ~(는/ㄴ)다 style has different non-past forms in verbs and adjectives. That is, verbs take ~는/ㄴ다 (~는다 after a consonant, ~ㄴ다 after a vowel) as in example (1), whereas adjectives and the copula ~이 take only ~다 as in (2) and (3). For the past tense, there is no variation between verbs and adjectives, both taking ~었/았/ㅆ다 as in (4).

3. It should be noted that there are both verbs and adjectives among ~하다 predicates. ~하다 verbs take ~는/ㄴ다 for their non-past forms, e.g., 공부한다, 하숙한다, 한국말을 한다, etc. On the other hand, ~하다 adjectives simply take ~다, as in 친절하다, 깨끗하다, etc., as in (5).

Tense marking in the plain ~다 style:

	Plain style (~다)	Polite style (~어요/아요)	Deferential style (~습니다/ㅂ니다)
Verb	~는다/ㄴ다	~어요	~습니다/ㅂ니다
Adjective	~다	~어요	~습니다/ㅂ니다
Copula	~(이)다	~이에요/예요	~입니다/ㅂ니다
Past	~었다/았다	~었/았어요	~었습니다/았습니다

Exercises

1. Convert the given sentences into the plain style.

    (1)   (i)   길을 건널 때 신호등을 잘 봐야 돼요.

              → 길을 건널 때 신호등을 잘 봐야 된다.

        (ii)   스티브는 지난주 학교 앞 하숙집으로 옮겼습니다.

              → 스티브는 지난주 학교 앞 하숙집으로 옮겼다.

(2)   집 열쇠를 잃어버려서 룸메이트를 기다리고 있어요.

(3)   내 남자 친구는 시간을 잘 안 지켜요.

(4)   학교 주차장이 넓어서 차를 많이 세울 수 있어요.

(5)   한국에서는 집 안에 들어갈 때 신발을 벗고 들어갑니다.

(6)   학교 앞에 있는 지하도로 길을 건넜어요.

(7)   인터넷에서 새 하숙집 약도를 찾아 봤어요.

(8)   차가 고장나서 지하철을 타고 학교에 갔습니다.

2. Convert the given narration into the polite ~어요/아요 style.

Example
        오늘은 민지와 함께 남산에 다녀왔다.
    → 오늘은 민지와 함께 남산에 다녀왔어요.

오늘은 민지와 함께 남산에 다녀왔다. 남산에 가려면 우리 학교 앞에서 지하철을 타고 명동역에서 내려서 15분쯤 걸어가면 된다. 남산 입구에 보면 케이블카(cable car)가 있는데 왕복 요금은 7,500원, 편도는 6,000원이다. 케이블카를 타고 올라가면 식당과 커피숍이 있는데 그곳에 유명한 서울타워(Seoul Tower)가 있다. 민지와 나는 엘리베이터를 타고 서울타워 위에 있는 식당에 가서 점심도 먹고 커피도 마셨다.

G6.2   The use of the plain style in speaking

Examples

(1)   [마크 and 동수 are waiting for a bus. 마크 sees a bus coming.]
       마크: 버스 온**다**!

(2)   [마크 has been looking for a file, and he sees it.]
       찾았**다**!

(3)   [마크 wants to take 민지 hiking tomorrow.]
       마크: 민지야, 너 내일 등산 갈 거**니**?

민지: 아니, 피곤해서 그냥 집에서 쉴까 해.
마크: 그러지 말고 같이 가**자**.
　　　 나 혼자 가면 재미없잖아.
민지: 그래, 좋아. 그럼 내일 아침에 전화할래?
마크: 알았어. 내일 보**자**. 시간 지**켜라**.

Notes

1. Occasionally, with slight modification in forms, the plain style, rather than the intimate ~어/아 style, is used when speaking to a child listener, to an intimate friend, or to a sibling.

2. Unlike the polite style and the intimate style, which do not have separate endings for different sentence types, the plain style uses different endings for different sentence types:

~다:	statement
~느냐/(으)냐/니:[a]	question
~어라/아라:[b]	command, request
~자:	proposal

a. In writing, verbs take ~느냐 and adjectives take ~(으)냐. In speaking, however, ~냐 or ~니 is used regardless of whether it is a verb or an adjective.

b. The ~어라/아라 variation is due to the same vowel harmony rule as for the ~어(요)/아(요) and ~어서/아서 variation.

3. There are some contexts that particularly call for the use of the plain style in conversation. The statement-ending ~다, for example, is used when the speaker wants to draw the listener's attention because the information is noteworthy or provoking, as in (1) and (2). As in (3), the question-ending ~니, the proposal-ending ~자, and the command-ending ~라 give a sense of more personal attachment to the conveyed message than the intimate ~어/아 style were used. With the question-ending ~니, for example, the speaker may show more of his/her curiosity or eagerness to know. The use of ~자 in making a proposal sounds more personal, affectionate, and appealing.

Exercises

1. Fill in the blank with the proper form of the plain style for the given verb.

(1)   A: 여기서는 택시 잡기 <u>힘드니</u> (힘들다)?

    B: 응. 큰 길로 <u>가 보자</u> (가 보다).

(2)   아버지: 민수 _____ (일어나다)?

    민지: 아직 안 일어났어요.

(3)   스티브:나 숙제 좀 보여 줄래?

    민지: 공부 좀 _____ (하다)! 숙제는 혼자 해야지.

        친구 거 빌리면 어떻게 _____ (하다)?

(4)   [스티브 is trying to figure out a puzzle. He finally finds the

    solution.]

    _____ (알다)!

(5)   스티브:동수야, 너 내일 등산 _____ (가다)?

    동수: 숙제 할 것도 있고 해서 집에서 쉴까 하는데.

    스티브:그러지 말고 같이 _____ (가다).

2. How would you say the following expressions in Korean? Choose an appropriate speech style (i.e., deferential, polite, intimate, or plain style) according to each context.

(1)   You are introducing yourself to an adult Korean speaker.

    "Glad to meet you." (Lit., "I am meeting you for the first

    time.")

    "I'm _____(your name)."

(2)   You are talking to a child.

    "What's your name? How old are you?"

(3)   You are being interviewed by a reporter from a Korean

    television station. The reporter compliments your Korean

language ability. How would you respond?

(4)   You are talking to a co-worker, "Let's go eat lunch."

(5)   You are asking a child, "Where is your father?"

(6)   You are calling your professor's office and say, "May I speak to Professor Kim please?"

G6.3	V.S.~기로 하다 'plan to/decide to'

Examples

(1)   A: 이번 여름 방학에 뭐 **하기로 했어요?**   What did you decide to do this summer break?

        B: 6월에 한국에 가**기로 했어요.**   I decided to go to Korea in June.

(2)   친구하고 등산 가**기로 했**는데 감기 때문에 못 갔어요.

(3)   A: 생일에 뭐 하**기로 했어요?**

        B: 저녁 먹고 나서 영화 보러 가**기로 했어요.**

(4)   A: 이번 학기에 졸업하지요?

        B: 아니요, 서두르지 않**기로 했어요.**

Notes

1. The construction [V.S.~기로 하다] expresses a decision or determination.

2. The negative form is expressed by 안 + verb + 기로 하다 or verb + 지 않기로 하다.

컴퓨터 게임을 안 하기로 했어요. = 컴퓨터 게임을 하지 않기로 했어요.

Exercises

1. Give an appropriate response using ~기로 하다.

(1)   A: 점심 먹었어요?

      B: 수잔 씨하고 두 시 반에 같이 <u>먹기로 했어요</u>.

(2)   주말에 뭐 하실 거예요?

      _____

(3)   수잔이랑 어디에서 만나기로 했어요?

      _____

(4)   크리스마스에 뭐 해요?

      _____

(5)   남자/여자 친구를 언제 또 만나요?

      _____

(6)   어머니날에 무슨 선물 살 거예요?

      _____

2. You are traveling with your friends. You came up with the following schedule. Compose a narrative using ~기로 하다.

겨울 방학 여행

1월 5일 (일)	인천국제공항 오후 4시 출발
1월 5일 (일)	뉴욕 케네디 공항 밤 9시 도착 (맨해튼 호텔)
1월 6일 (월)	오후 6시 브로드웨이 쇼 (show)
1월 7일 (화)	나이아가라 폭포 (fall)
1월 8일 (수)	토론토 다운타운에서 쇼핑
1월 9일 (목)	케네디 공항 출발

3. Do you make New Year's resolutions? Say three things you decided to do and three things you decided not to do this year.

(1)   올해는 매일 일기를 쓰기로 했어요.

(2)   _____

(3)   _____

(4)   _____

(5)   올해는 담배를 피우지 않기로 했어요.

(6)   _____

(7)   _____

(8)   _____

Conversation 2   관악산 입구까지 가 주세요.

(스티브가 지하철역에서 표 파는 곳을 찾고 있다.)

스티브: 저어, 실례지만, 말씀 좀 묻겠습니다.
          여기 표 파는 곳이 어디 있어요?

여자: 지금 매표소는 복잡하니까
          저기 발매기에서 사세요.

스티브: 네, 감사합니다.

(스티브가 서울대입구역에서 내려서 택시를 잡으려고 손을 흔든다.)

기사: 손님, 어디까지 가세요?

스티브: 관악산 입구요.

기사: 네, 알겠습니다.

스티브: 길이 많이 막히네요.

기사: 등산객이 많아서 그래요. 라디오에서 이번 주에
          단풍이 제일 아름답다고 하네요.^{G6.4}

스티브:　아, 그래요? 제가 운이 좋은 것 같네요.

기사:　몇 시까지 가셔야 되는데요?

스티브:　10시까지요.

기사:　아무리 서둘러도[G6.5] 10시까지는 힘들겠는데요.

COMPREHENSION QUESTIONS

1. 스티브는 표를 어디서 사야 합니까?
2. 스티브는 지하철을 타고 어디까지 갑니까?
3. 관악산 입구까지 어떻게 갑니까?
4. 스티브는 몇 시까지 관악산 입구에 가야 합니까?
5. 관악산 가는 길이 왜 막힙니까?

NEW WORDS

NOUN		환승(하다)	transfer
경찰	police	횡단보도	crosswalk
고속도로	highway, freeway	**VERB**	
공사	construction	(사고) 나다	to happen, occur
교통카드	transportation card	늘다	to improve
도움	help	모이다	to gather
등산객	mountain climber	이용하다	to utilize
마을 버스	town shuttle bus	즐기다	to enjoy
매표소	ticket office	**ADJECTIVE**	
발매기	vending machine	외롭다	to be lonely
사고	accident	위험하다	to be dangerous
술	alcoholic beverage	**ADVERB**	
운	luck, fortune	거의	almost
인도	sidewalk	**SUFFIX**	
자연	nature	~다/라/자/냐고 하다	say that
장소	place, location	아무리 ~어/아도	no matter how
차도	street, road		
(교통) 표지판	(traffic) sign		

NEW EXPRESSIONS

In 제가 운이 좋은 것 같아요, the expression 운이 좋다 [Lit., 'the luck is good'.] means 'be lucky, fortunate; to have good luck'. The noun 운 'luck' can be used in the following ways:

저는 운이 좋아요.	I have good luck.
제가 운이 있어요.	I have luck; I am lucky.
철수는 운이 별로 안 좋아요.	Cheolsu doesn't have good luck.
올해는 제가 운이 나빠요.	This year, I have bad luck.

G6.4	Indirect quotation: ~다고 하다, ~(으/느)냐고 하다, ~(으)라고 하다, ~자고 하다

Examples

Statement: ~(는/ㄴ)다고 하다/~(이)라고 하다
(1)   마크: 여보세요. 동수 좀 부탁합니다.
        누나: 동수 아직 안 들어왔는데요.   동수 hasn't come home yet.
                오늘 좀 늦는**다고 했어요.**   *He said that* he would be
                                            a little late today.

        마크: 저 마크인데요, 동수
                들어오면 제가 전화했**다고**
                전해 주세요.

(2)   요즘 공사 때문에 길이 막힌**다고 한다**.

(3)   제임스는 대학원생**이라고 했어요**.

Request: ~(으)라고 하다/~지 말라고 하다
(4)   고속도로에서 운전할 때는 표지판을 잘 보**라고 한다**.

(5)   선생님이 수업에 늦지 말**라고 하셨다**.

(6)   경찰이 차도 말고 횡단보도를 이용하**라고 했다**.

Proposal: ~자고 하다

(7)   동수가 친구들에게 한국 음식을 먹**자고 했다**.

(8)   동수가 영미한테 여행을 가**자고 했다**.

Question: ~(으/느)냐고 하다/묻나

(9)   동수가 나한테 언제 미국에 가**냐고 했다**.

(10)   직원한테 어디서 기차를 타**느냐고 물었다**.

Notes

1. Indirect quotation is used when the speaker quotes what somebody else said or when the speaker passes his/her or someone else's thought to the listener. It takes the various forms of [QUOTED MESSAGE]고 하다.

(i)   . . .고 해/해요/한다/합니다 when quoting a general message that is currently going around

(ii)   . . .고 했어/했어요/했다/했습니다 when quoting a specific message that was said in the past

(iii) . . .고 하셔/하세요/하신다/하십니다 in the present tense, . . .고 하셨어/하셨어요/하셨다/하셨습니다 in the past tense when the quoted message is/was said by someone who is respected (i.e., the honorific forms of 하다 are used)

(iv)   In colloquial speech, especially in Seoul, the indirect quotation takes the verb 그래(요)/그랬어(요) instead of 해요/했어(요). Also, the quotation particle 고 is often deleted in colloquial speech. For example,

마크: 여보세요, 동수 좀 바꿔 주세요.
동수 누나: 동수 아직 안 들어 왔는데요.
             오늘 좀 늦는다(고) 그랬어요.

2. The quoted message itself also takes different endings of the plain style depending on the sentence type of the quoted message, — that is, whether it is a statement, question, command, or proposal, — and on the time of the event in the quoted message.

(i)   ~(는/ㄴ/었)다고 하다 when the quoted message is a statement

V~는다고 하다 with a verb whose stem ends in a consonant

V~ㄴ다고 하다 with a verb stem ending in a vowel

A~다고 하다 with an adjective

~라고 하다 with the copula ~이

V/A~었/았다고 하다 when the event in the quoted message occurred prior to the actual saying of the message.

(ii)   ~느냐/(으)냐/었느냐고 하다 when the quoted message is a question

V~느냐고 하다 with a verb

A~(으)냐고 하다 with an adjective and the copula

V/A~었았/느냐고 하다

(iii) ~(으)라고 하다 when the quoted message is a command or request. Note that ~(으)라 is used instead of ~어라/아라 of the plain style.

(iv)   ~자고 하다 when the quoted message is a proposal.

	Standard	Colloquial
Statement		
	V~는/ㄴ다고 해(요)/했어(요)	~는/ㄴ다(고) 그래(요)/그랬어(요)
	A~다고 해(요)/했어(요)	~다(고) 그래(요)/그랬어(요)
	~었/다고 해(요)/했어(요)	~었/다고 그래(요)/그랬어(요)
Question		
	V~느냐고 해(요)/했어(요)	~느냐 그래(요))/그랬어(요)
	A~(으)냐고 해(요)/했어(요)	~(으)냐 그래(요))/그랬어(요)
	~었/았느냐고 해(요)/했어(요)	~었/았느냐 그래(요))/그랬어(요)
Command/Request/Proposal		
	V~(으)라고 해(요)/했어(요)	~(으)라 그래(요)/그랬어(요)
	V~자고 해(요)/했어(요)	~자 그래(요)/그랬어(요)

3. The act of saying may be indicated by a different verb than 하다 if the specific nature of saying is to be specified, as in (1) and (10):

~다/라고 전해 주다   Convey/pass along the message that . . .

~느냐/(으)냐고 물어보다   Ask if/whether . . .

Sample conjugations of indirect discourse

			Present tense	Past tense
V e r b s	Statement	먹다	먹는다고 했어요/그랬어요	먹었다고 했어요/그랬어요
	Question		먹느냐고 했어요/그랬어요	먹었느냐고 했어요/그랬어요
	Command		먹으라고 했어요/그랬어요	
	Proposal		먹자고 했어요/그랬어요	
	Statement	사다	산다고 했어요/그랬어요	샀다고 했어요/그랬어요
	Question		사느냐고 했어요/그랬어요	샀느냐고 했어요/그랬어요
	Command		사라고 했어요/그랬어요	
	Proposal		사자고 했어요/그랬어요	
A d j e c t i v e s	Statement	좋다	좋다고 했어요/그랬어요	좋았다고 했어요/그랬어요
	Question		좋으냐고 했어요/그랬어요	좋았느냐고 했어요/그랬어요
	Statement	예쁘다	예쁘다고 했어요/그랬어요	예뻤다고 했어요/그랬어요
	Question		예쁘냐고 했어요/그랬어요	예뻤느냐고 했어요/그랬어요

4. The indirect quotation ~다고 해요/그래요 is similar to the hearsay expression ~대(요)/래(요) in that the speaker conveys somebody else's message or thought. The difference between the two is that the main purpose of the hearsay expression ~대(요)/래(요), as in 스티브가 자고 있대요, is to convey the content of the message itself, often even without revealing who the primary speaker is, whereas the main purpose of the indirect quotation ~다고 해요/그래요 is to quote someone's speech.

Exercises

1. Using the indirect quotation form, make up an utterance according to the given context.

    (1)   [동수: 누나, 나 오늘 좀 늦을 거야.]
        스티브: 여보세요, 동수 좀 부탁합니다.
        동수누나: 동수 아직 안 들어 왔는데요.
            <u>오늘 좀 늦는다고 했어요.</u>

    (2)   [민지: 스티브, 나 수업 끝날 때까지 기다려.]
        동수: 스티브, 빨리 가자.
        스티브: 먼저 가. 나 민지 기다려야 돼.

            _____

    (3)   [스티브: 오늘 차 사고가 나서 학교에 못 가요.]
        동수: 누나, 나한테 전화온 데 없어요?
        동수 누나: 스티브한테서 전화 왔는데,

            _____

    (4)   [스티브: 누나, 동수 내일 몇 시에 학교에 가요?
        동수 누나: 잘 모르겠는데.]
        동수: 누나, 혹시 스티브가 전화 안 했어요?
        동수 누나: 응, 아까 스티브한테서 전화 왔는데,
            내일 _____

    (5)   [우진: 저 미국에서 온 우진이라고 하는데요.
            동수 좀 바꿔 주세요]
        누나: 동수야, 전화 받어.

            _____

(6)   [민지: 스티브, 내일 등산 나하고 같이 가.]

       동수: 민지도 내일 등산 같이 가니?

       스티브: 응, 어제 전화 왔는데,

       _____

2. Change into an indirect quotation.

(1)   "자전거는 인도 말고 차도에서 타세요."

     자전거는 인도 말고 차도에서 타라고 했습니다.

(2)   "밖에서 잠깐만 기다리세요."

     _____

(3)   "방금 라디오에서 뉴스 들었어요?"

     _____

(4)   "술 마시고 운전하지 마세요."

     _____

(5)   "날씨도 좋은데 운동하러 공원에 갑시다."

     _____

(6)   "이번 토요일에 다 같이 모이자."

     _____

(7)   "수업 시간에 졸지 말고 공부하세요."

     _____

(8)   "비가 오니까 우산 가지고 가세요."

     _____

3. Complete the following dialogues using the indirect quotation form ~고 하다.

(1)   A: 왜 택시 안 타고 지하철을 타세요?

       B: 동수가 토요일은 길이 복잡하니까 지하철 타라고

           했어요.

(2)   A: 이번 토요일에 같이 등산 갈래요?

B: 일기예보에서 이번 토요일에 _____

A: 그래요? 그럼 안 되겠네요.

(3)   A: 민지 씨 왜 안 와요?

B: 아침에 중요한 약속이 있어서 늦게 _____

(4)   A: 마크 씨가 한국에 온 지 1년이나 됐어요.

B: 그래요? 나한테는 6개월밖에 _____

(5)   A: 동수 씨 어제 민지 생일파티에 갔어요?

B: 아마 갔을 거예요. 어제 집에 가다가 만났는데

G6.5   아무리 ~어도/아도 'no matter how . . .'

Examples

(1)   지하철역에서 내려서 도봉산   I got off at the subway
가는 마을버스를 기다리는데,   station and then waited for
아무리 기다려도 오지 않아서   a town shuttle bus going to
택시를 탔다.   Dobong Mountain. Although
                                   I waited a long time, the bus
                                   didn't come, so I took a taxi.

(2)   [민지 and 동수 are looking up a word in a dictionary.]
민지: 동수 씨, 아직도 못 찾았어요?
동수: 네, **아무리 찾아도** 못 찾겠어요.
       민지씨가 한 번 찾아 봐요.

(3)   동수: 민지 씨, 스티브한테 연락했어요?
민지: **아무리 전화해도** 안 받는데요.

(4)   동수: 스티브 씨, 파티에 올 거예요?
스티브:글쎄요. **아무리 생각해 봐도** 못 갈 것 같아요.

Notes

1. 아무리 ~어도/아도 is used when the intended goal could not be obtained even after maximum effort has been made. Hence, it is typically (but not always) followed by a negative expression indicating the failure to obtain the intended goal or effect.

2. The ~어도/아도 variation is the same as that of ~어요/아요, ~어서/아서, ~었/았-, etc.

Exercise

Using 아무리 ~어도/아도, make up a dialogue according to the given context.

(1) 민지: 여기 음식 참 많이 주지요?

　　동수: 네. <u>아무리 먹어도</u> 끝이 안 나네요.

(2) 민지: 스티브 씨, 날씨가 추운데 등산가실 거예요?

　　스티브:네, _____ 등산 갈 거예요.

(3) 소연: 스티브 씨, 왜 그렇게 많이 먹어요?

　　스티브:네, 하루 종일 식사를 못 해서요,

　　_____ 배가 고파요.

(4) 민지: 어제 동수 씨 오래 기다렸어요?

　　스티브:네, 약속 장소에서 _____ 오지

　　않아서 그냥 집에 갔어요.

(5) 동수: 아니, 민지 씨, 스티브 씨하고 같이 오기로 하지

　　않았어요?

　　민지: 네. 근데 스티브 씨한테 _____

　　안 받아서 그냥 혼자 왔어요.

(6) 아무리 친구가 _____ 외로워요.

(7) A: 한국어를 정말 잘하시네요.

　　B: 아니에요. 아무리 _____ 한국어가

　　안 늘어요.

Narration | 스티브의 일기

10월 30일 토요일

오늘은 아주 맑은 가을 날씨였다. 그래서 동수와
관악산으로 등산을 갔다 왔다. 관악산에 가려면 우리 학교
앞에서 서울대입구역까지 먼저 지하철을 타고 간 다음
버스로 갈아타야 한다. 서울에서는 교통 카드를 사용하면
지하철과 버스를 무료로 환승할 수 있다. 그런데, 어제 교통
카드를 잃어버려서 오늘은 그냥 승차권을 샀다. 매표소가
복잡해서 어떤 아주머니의 도움으로 발매기에서 표를 샀다.
지하철을 타고 서울대입구역에서 내렸는데 길이 복잡해서
관악산으로 가는 버스 정류장을 못 찾았다. 그래서 택시를 탔는데 길이 많이 막혀서 약속 장소에 10분 늦게 도착했다.
약속 시간을 못 지켜서 동수에게 미안했다. 오래간만에
복잡한 도시를 떠나서 자연을 즐길 수 있어서 좋았다.

COMPREHENSION QUESTIONS

1. 어느 계절입니까?
2. 관악산에는 어떻게 갑니까?
3. 스티브는 왜 승차권을 샀습니까?
4. 스티브는 어디서 표를 샀습니까?
5. 스티브는 왜 늦었습니까?

CULTURE

주민등록증

미국에는 사회보장번호
(Social Security number)가
있고 한국에는 주민등록번호
(Resident Registration number)
가 있다. 주민등록번호는 모두
13자리의 숫자로 되어 있는데,
앞의 여섯 자리는 생년월일을
나타낸다. 예를 들어 1995년 8월 24일 생의 주민등록 번호 앞자리는
950824가 된다. 뒤의 일곱자리 중 첫 자리는 성별을 나타낸다. 남자는 1
(950824-1XXXXXX) 혹은 3, 여자는 2 혹은 4가 된다(950824-2XXXXXX).
그래서 주민등록번호를 보면 그 사람의 나이와 성별을 쉽게 알 수 있다.
모든 사람들의 주민등록 번호가 다르기 때문에, 주민등록번호는 본인
확인이 필요할 경우 많이 쓰인다. 신용카드나 은행 계좌를 만들 때 그리고
새로 핸드폰을 사서 쓸 때도 주민등록번호가 필요하다.

한국에서 오래 사는 외국인들의 경우에는 외국인등록번호(Alien Registration number)를 받게 된다.

나타내다	to show, represent	숫자	number
본인 확인	self-identification	쓰이다	to be used
생년월일	date of birth	예를 들어	for example
성별	sex	자리	digit

USAGE

1. Asking for and giving directions

Examples

(1) A: 저어, 실례지만, 말씀 좀 묻겠습니다.
         여기 표 사는 곳이 어디 있어요?
     B: 어디까지 가세요?
     A: "관악역"이요.
     B: 외국분 같은데 제가 도와 드릴게요. 이쪽으로 오세요.
     A: 감사합니다.
     B: 뭘요.

(2) A: 저어, 실례합니다.
     B: 네.
     A: 시청까지 바로 가는 버스 있어요?
     B: 바로 가는 건 없고 18번을 타고 가다가
         6번으로 갈아타야 돼요.
     A: 감사합니다.

When you ask for directions on the street, you can start by saying something like "저어, 실례합니다. 말씀 좀 묻겠습니다." (저어, as a conversation opener, expresses hesitation.)

[Exercise 1] Converse with your partner on the following topics.

> (1)   지금 어디 사세요?
>
> (2)   주소가 어떻게 돼요?
>
> (3)   학교에서 어떻게 가는지 약도 좀 그려 주실래요?

[Exercise 2] You are invited to your friend's house for Thanksgiving dinner. You need to get directions to your friend's place. Take the roles of both parties.

[Exercise 3] Your Korean teacher invites you to a barbecue. Call the teacher to get the directions to his/her place from the classroom and draw a map. Then compare your map with that of others.

Useful words for city guide (도시 안내)

시청 (city hall)	경찰서 (a police station)
소방서 (a fire station)	박물관 (a museum)
모텔/호텔 (an inn/hotel)	공장 (a factory)
상점/가게 (a store)	제과점/빵집 (a bakery)
노래방 (a karaoke room)	술집 (a pub, a bar)
세탁소 (a laundry)	이발소 (a barbershop)
미용실 (a beauty salon)	동물원 (a zoo)
고층빌딩 (a high-rise building)	간판 (store signs)
차도 (a road for vehicles)	인도 (a sidewalk)
신호등 (a traffic signal)	시내 (downtown)
네거리/사거리 (intersection)	주유소 (a gas station)
버스 정류장 (a bus stop)	지하철 입구 (a subway entrance)
상가 (the business section)	지하 상가 (an underground market)
방송국 (a broadcasting station)	신문사 (a newspaper publisher)

2. Using public transportation

Examples

(1)   (택시 타기)
       기사: 손님, 어디로 모실까요?
       마크: 도봉산 입구까지 가 주세요.

(2)   (택시 안에서)
       기사: 도봉산 입구에 거의 다 왔는데, 어디 세워 드릴까요?
       마크: 저기 신호등 지나서 지하도 입구에서 세워 주세요.
       기사: 알겠습니다.
       마크: (택시 미터기를 보면서) 여기 2,500원 있습니다.
       기사: 감사합니다. 안녕히 가세요.

(3)   (기차역에서)
       A: 서울-부산 왕복 하나 주세요.
       B: 창가 자리로 드릴까요, 복도 쪽으로 드릴까요?
       A: 창가 쪽으로 주세요. 얼마예요?
       B: 만오천 원입니다.
       (기차역 train station, 창가 자리 a window seat, 복도 an aisle seat)

Expressions that you hear from a taxi driver:

       어디까지 가세요? / 어디로 모실까요?
       어디 세워 드릴까요?

Telling the destination:

       _____(destination)에 가 주세요.
       _____(destination)~(이)요.
       _____(location)에 세워 주세요.

Asking for the taxi fare:

       얼마예요?
       얼마 나왔어요?
       얼마 드리면 돼요?

Making a request:

       아저씨, 시간이 없으니까 좀 더 빨리 가 주세요.
       위험하니까 천천히 가 주세요.

[Exercise 1] Suppose you are learning Korean in 서울. You want to visit 경주 by train next Saturday. You need a round-trip train ticket from 서울 to 경주. Take the roles of the customer and a clerk at a ticket counter.

3. Making telephone calls

Examples

(1) Taking and leaving a message

영미:	여보세요, 우진이 집에 있어요?
우진 형:	없는데요. 오늘 좀 늦는다고 했어요.
영미:	저, 우진이 친구 영미라고 하는데요.
	우진이 들어오면 영미가 전화했다고 좀 전해 주세요.
우진 형:	네, 그러죠.
영미:	고맙습니다. 안녕히 계세요.

(2) Returning a telephone call

우진:	영미, 나야, 아까 전화했다면서? 무슨 일이야?
영미:	응, 숙제를 하다가 모르는 게 있어서 전화했는데,
	내일 학교에서 좀 만날 수 있어?
우진:	그래. 몇 시에 만날까?
영미:	아침 10시 도서관 앞에서 어때?
우진:	응, 좋아. 마침 나도 그 때 수업이 없으니까 잘 됐네.
영미:	고마워, 그럼 내일 도서관 앞에서 만나.
우진:	응, 그래. 끊어.

(3) Wrong numbers

A:	여보세요.
B:	여보세요. 최성호 씨 좀 부탁합니다.
A:	여기 그런 사람 없는데요. 몇 번에 거셨어요?
B:	거기 567-7890 아니에요?
A:	아닌데요. 전화 잘못 거셨어요. 여긴 7895예요.
B:	죄송합니다.

Useful expressions

통화 중이에요.	The line is busy.
전화 잘못 거셨어요.	You have the wrong number.
지역 번호가 뭐예요?	What is the area code?
자동 응답기에 메시지를	Please leave a message on the
남겨 주세요.	answering machine.
전화가 고장 났어요.	The phone is out of order.
잠깐만 기다리세요./잠깐만요.	Hold on please.
전화기	the telephone (machine) set
장거리 전화	a long-distance call
전화 회사	a telephone company
국제 전화	an international call
전화비	a telephone bill
전화를 걸다/끊다	to call/to hang up

[Exercise 1] Converse with your partner about the following questions.

(1) 한국말로 전화해 본 적이 있으세요?

(2) 전화기를 혼자 쓰세요? 아니면 다른 사람이랑 같이 쓰세요?

(3) 집에 전화기가 몇 대 있으세요? 어디 어디 있어요?

(4) 누구한테 전화를 제일 자주 하세요? 얼마나 자주
     전화하세요?

(5) 전화하는 걸 좋아하세요?

(6) 어느 장거리 전화 회사를 사용하세요? 왜요?

(7) 한 달에 전화비가 얼마나 나와요?

[Exercise 2] Practice the following telephone conversation.

영미:	여보세요, 저 우진이 친구 영미라고 하는데요. 우진이 있으면 좀 부탁합니다.
우진 형:	아직 학교에서 안 돌아왔는데요.
영미:	우진이 들어오면 영미가 전화했다고 좀 전해 주시겠어요?
우진 형:	네, 그러죠.
영미:	고맙습니다. 안녕히 계세요.

Practice the above conversation again, substituting the underlined part with the following messages.

(1)   영미 is in the library now.

(2)   영미 is waiting for 우신 in front of the library.

(3)   영미 already went home.

(4)   영미 called to invite 우진 to her birthday party.

(5)   영미 called to ask when the Korean test will take place.

[Exercise 3] Someone just dialed your number by mistake. Make a dialogue.

[Exercise 4] With your classmate, make a telephone dialogue using the intimate speech style for the following situations.

(1)   You missed Korean class today because you had a cold. You call your classmate James to find out about any assignment due. James says that there is no homework for tomorrow, but there will be a quiz on lesson 5 tomorrow.

(2)   You have to go to the airport tomorrow morning to pick up your parents. You are going to miss Korean class. You ask your classmate to tell your Korean teacher that you will turn in your homework the day after tomorrow.

[Exercise 5] You call to talk with 영미. She is not home. Leave a voice message for her to call you back; give the time and your phone number.

[Exercise 6] Your younger sister's friend (수미) calls to speak with your sister (영희). She is not home. Take a message.

4. Writing a journal

Example

10월 20일 토요일 (날씨: 아주 맑음)

오늘은 아주 화창한 가을 날씨였다. 시험이 끝나서 같은 반 친구들이
도봉산으로 등산을 가자고 했다. 전에 도봉산 쪽으로 가 본 적이 없어서
동수한테 교통편을 물어 보았다. 동수는 나한테 지하철을 타고 도봉역까지
가서 거기서부터는 도봉산 행 버스를 타라고 가르쳐 주었다.

나는 동수 말대로 가까운 지하철역으로 내려가서 어느 아주머니의
도움으로 자동 발매기에서 표를 산 다음 도봉역에서 내렸다. 그런데 아무리
기다려도 도봉산으로 가는 버스가 오지 않았다. 약속 시간에 늦을 것 같아서
택시를 탔는데 다행히 약속 시간에 맞추어 도착했다. 오래간만에 복잡한
도시를 떠나서 친구들과 마음껏 하루를 즐길 수 있었다.

The plain speech style is usually used in journals.

[Exercise 1] Write a journal entry about your past weekend using the
plain speech style. (Challenge: Read your journal to the class.)

Lesson 6. Public Transportation

CONVERSATION 1: Are you all prepared for hiking?
(Dongsoo makes a call to Steve's cell phone.)

Dongsoo: Oh, Steve, I'm sorry. I couldn't answer the phone before because the battery had gone out.

Steve: Oh, that's all right. I called because we decided to go hiking to Gwanak Mountain this weekend, you know. But Woojin is not likely to go since an important thing suddenly came up for this weekend.

Dongsoo: Is that so? It's too bad. It would be nice if he could go as well. But we cannot help it. Are you all prepared to hike?

Steve: Yes. By the way, is there a bus that goes directly from the front of the school to Gwanak Mountain?

Dongsoo: No bus goes directly; you have to transfer on the way. First take a subway to the Seoul University Station; there, transfer to a bus.

Steve: I got it. I'll see you this Saturday morning at the entrance to Gwanak Mountain.

CONVERSATION 2: Please go to the entrance to Gwanak Mountain.
(Steve is looking for a place to buy a ticket at the subway station.)

Steve: Excuse me, may I ask a question? Where is the place that sells tickets here?

Woman: Buy a ticket from the vending machine over there because the ticket office is crowded now.

Steve: Okay, thank you.

(Steve gets off at the Seoul University Station and waves his hand to catch a taxi.)

Driver: Sir, where are you going?

Steve: To the entrance to Gwanak Mountain.

Driver: Okay, I got it.

Steve: The road is really congested.
Driver: That is because there are many mountain hikers. People
              say that the autumn foliage is the most beautiful this week.
Steve: Oh, is that so? I think I am lucky.
Driver: By what time should you get there?
Steve: By 10 o'clock.
Driver: No matter how much we hurry, it will be hard to get there
              by 10 o'clock.

NARRATION: Steve's diary

October 30, Saturday

Today the autumn weather was very clear, so I went hiking up Gwanak
Mountain with Dongsoo. To go to Gwanak Mountain, one has to take
a subway in front of the school to the Seoul University Station and
transfer to a bus. In Seoul, it is free to transfer from a subway to a bus if
you use a transportation card. However, since I lost my transportation
card yesterday, I just bought a ticket. The ticket office was crowded, so I
bought a ticket from a vending machine with the help of a lady. I took a
subway and got off at the Seoul University Station, but I couldn't find the
bus stop to Gwanak Mountain because the roads were complicated. Thus,
I took a taxi, but I arrived at the appointed place ten minutes late because
the road was really congested. I felt sorry for Dongsoo because I didn't
meet him at the appointed time. It was nice to leave the crowded city after
a long while and enjoy nature.

CULTURE: 주민등록증

The Resident Registration number in Korea is similar to the Social
Security number in America. The Resident Registration number is
composed of thirteen digits, of which the first six represent the person's
birthday. For example, the first six digits for someone who was born
on August 24, 1995, are 950824. The first digit of the other seven digits
represents gender: 1 or 3 for male and 2 or 4 for female. Therefore, you
can figure out a person's age and gender easily by just looking at the

Resident Registration number. Since everybody's number is unique, the number is often used when identification is needed. You need the Resident Registration number when you get credit cards or open bank accounts and when you want to buy a new cell phone and start the phone service. Foreigners who live in Korea for a long time receive an Alien Registration number.

7과 가게에서 [At a Store]

Conversation 1 사과 한 상자에 얼마예요?

(우진이는 과일을 사러 동네 과일 가게에 갔다.)

우진: 안녕하세요, 아주머니.

주인: 어, 학생, 오래간만이에요. 그동안 어디
　　　다녀왔어요?

우진: 네, 방학 동안 미국 집에 갔다 왔어요.

주인: 그랬어요?

우진: 와, 과일이 맛있어 보이네요.^{G7.1}
　　　요즘 어떤 과일이 잘 팔려요?^{G7.2}

주인: 사과하고 배가 잘 팔리는 편이에요

우진: 사과는 한 상자에 얼마예요?

주인: 이만 원이에요.

우진: 한 상자에 몇 개나 들어 있어요?^{G7.3}

주인: 열 개 들어 있어요.

우진: 이 귤도 맛있겠네요. 귤은 얼마예요?

주인: 세 개에 천원이에요.

우진: 그럼 귤은 삼천 원어치만 주세요.

COMPREHENSION QUESTIONS

1. 우진이는 방학에 무엇을 했습니까?
2. 요즘은 어떤 과일이 잘 팔립니까?
3. 우진이는 사과 한 상자에 얼마입니까?
4. 우진이는 귤을 얼마어치 샀습니까?

NEW WORDS

NOUN		VERB	
거스름돈	change (money)	깎다	to cut down
과일	fruit	다녀 오다	to go and get back
귤	tangerine	닫히다	to be closed
도둑	thief	물다	to bite
두부	tofu	물리다	to be bitten
배	pear	뺏기다	to be deprived of
사과	apple	열리다	to be open
생선	fish	잡히다	to be caught
소리	sound, noise	팔리다	to be sold
약	medicine	**ADJECTIVE**	
우체부	postman	행복하다	to be happy
편의점	convenience store	**SUFFIX**	
PRONOUN		어치	worth, value
누가	someone	~어/아 보이다	to appear, look
뭐	something	~어/아 있다	to be in the state of
어디	somewhere		
언제	sometime		

NEW EXPRESSIONS

어치 'worth' is a suffix that attaches to an amount. Following are some
examples.

천 원어치   an amount that is worth 1,000 won
얼마어치   how much (in money)

사과 얼마어치 드릴까요?   How much worth of apples
                                        do you want?
오천 원어치만 주세요.   Just give me 5,000 won's worth.

GRAMMAR

G7.1   ~어/아 보이다 'someone/something appears . . ., looks . . .'

Examples

(1)   스티브:민지 씨, 헤어스타일이 바뀌었네요.
                    민지 씨 얼굴하고 잘 어울리는데요.
            민지: 네, 스티브 씨도 머리 깎으니까 시원**해 보여요**.

(2)   스시가 맛있**어 보여요**. The sushi looks delicious.

(3)   구두가 멋있**어 보여요**. Those shoes look cool.

(4)   제인: 이 생선 어때요?
                    괜찮**아 보여요**?
            제프: 네, 싱싱**해 보이**는데요.

(5)   무거**워 보이**는데 도와 드릴까요?

(6)   자동차가 비**싸 보여요**.

Notes

1. ~어/아 보이다 is used when commenting about the surface appearance
of something; the speaker does not claim that the statement is factual.

2. ~어/아 보이다 is attached only to adjectives.

Citation form	Gloss	~어/아요	~어/아 보여요
시원하다	to be refreshing, cool	시원해요	시원해 보여요
싱싱하다	to be fresh	싱싱해요	싱싱해 보여요
무겁다	to be heavy	무거워요	무거워 보여요
맛있다	to be tasty	맛있어요	맛있어 보여요
멋있다	to be fancy, stylish, cool	멋있어요	멋있어 보여요
비싸다	to be expensive	비싸요	비싸 보여요

Exercise

1. Choosing from the given vocabulary, give a statement of appearance based on the given cue.

행복하다, 건강하다, 기분이 좋다, 기분이 나쁘다, 춥다, 시원하다

    (1)   [스티브가 머리를 깎았어요.] 시원해 보여요.

    (2)   [동수가 지갑을 잃어버렸어요.]_____

    (3)   [민지는 운동히 열심히 했어요.]_____

    (4)   [스티브는 입술이 파래요.]_____

    (5)   [제니는 지난 주에 결혼했어요.]_____

G7.2   Passive verbs

Examples

(1)   우진: 요즘 어떤 옷이 유행이에요?
          점원: 요즘은 밝은 색 옷이 잘 **팔려**요.

(2)   기사: 어디 세워 드릴까요?
          스티브:저기 신호등 **보이**지요? 저 신호등 지나서 세워 주세요.

(3)   동생한테 좋아하는 시계를 **뺏겼**어요.
    I had my favorite watch taken away by my younger sister.

(4)   A: 무슨 소리가 났는데 못 들었어요?
               I heard a sound. Didn't you hear it?
        B: 바람에 문이 **닫히**는 소리예요.
               It's the sound of the door being closed by the wind.

(5)   도둑이 경찰한테 **잡혔**다. The thief was caught by the police.

Notes

1. A situation is typically described from the point of view of the actor of an action. A situation may occasionally be described, however, from the point of view of the object of an action.

In English, passive forms are used for that purpose (e.g., The door is being opened/closed. The thief was caught by the police yesterday.) The passive construction in English is made grammatically by using the copula 'be' along with the past participle form of the verb (e.g., to be opened). In Korean, the passive construction is made with the suffix ~이, ~히, ~리, or ~기 attached to a verb stem, creating a new word.

> 개가 우체부를 물었어요 (물다).
> A dog bit the postman.

> 우체부가 개한테 물렸어요 (물+리+다 → 물리다).
> The postman was bitten by a dog.

2. Passives are used more often in English than in Korean. In English, almost all transitive verbs can be made into passives. In Korean, however, only a limited number of transitive verbs can be made passive.

3. Which verb is subject to this passive verb formation, as well as which verb takes which suffix among ~이, ~히, ~리, and ~기, simply has to be learned. We will classify them by the suffix a verb stem takes.

Active	Passive	Example
(i) ~이 types		
보다 to see (신호등을 못 봤어요.)	보이다	저기 신호등(이) 보이지요? Can you see the traffic light over there?
쓰다 to use (이 꽃 결혼식에 쓸 거예요?)	쓰이다	이 꽃은 결혼식에 잘 쓰여요. This flower is often used for weddings.

Active	Passive	Example
(ii) ~히 types		
닫다 to close (문 좀 닫아 주세요.)	닫히다	바람에 문이 저절로 닫혔어요. The door was closed by the wind.
막다 to block (경찰이 길을 막았어요.)	막히다	차가 너무 많아서 길이 막혔어요. Because there were too many cars, traffic was blocked.
잡다 to catch (경찰이 도둑을 잡았어요)	잡히다	도둑이 경찰한테 잡혔어요. The thief was caught by the police.

Active	Passive	Example
(iii) ~리 types		
물다 to bite (개가 우체부 다리를 물었어요.)	물리다	우체부는 개한테 다리를 물렸어요. The mail carrier was bitten by a dog on his/her leg.
열다 to open (이 가게 언제 열어요?)	열리다	가게가 열렸어요. The store has been opened.
듣다 to hear (라디오 자주 들으세요?)	들리다	우리 라디오가 잘 안 들려요. Our radio cannot be heard.
팔다 to sell (요새 집 많이 파세요?)	팔리다	요새는 집이 잘 안 팔려요. These days houses are not sold often.

Active	Passive	Example
(iv) ~기 types		
뺏다 to take away from (오빠가 동생 사과를 뺏었어요.)	뺏기다	오빠한테 사과를 뺏겼어요. She had her apple taken away by her brother.
안다 to hold, hug (엄마가 아이를 안았습니다)	안기다	아이가 엄마한테 안겼습니다. The baby was held by Mom.
쫓다 to chase (개가 고양이를 쫓습니다.)	쫓기다	고양이가 개한테 쫓기고 있습니다. The cat is being chased by the dog.

4. With active verbs, actors are marked, if necessary, with the subject particle 이/가 or the topic particle 은/는, whereas the objects are marked with the object particle 을/를. With passive verbs, it is the objects that are marked with either the subject particle 이/가 or the topic particle 은/는, and the actors or instigators are marked, if necessary, with the dative particle 한테 if animate, 에 if inanimate.

Exercise

Fill in the blank with the appropriate form of a verb, active or passive. Choose the proper verb from the given list, based on the given context.

팔다   열다   닫다   보다   듣다   뺏다

(1)   우진: 요즘 어떤 옷이 유행이에요?

       점원: 요즘은 밝은 색 옷이 잘 팔려요.

(2)   A: 어디서 좋은 클래식 음악이 _____는데요.

       B: 클래식 음악 자주 _____?

       A: 네, 자주 들어요.

(3)   A: 무슨 소리예요?

       B: 문이 바람에 _____ 소리예요.

(4)   A: 동수가 안 _____. 어디 갔어요?

       B: 가게에 두부 사러 나갔어요.

(5)   A: 이 가방 좋은데요. 어디서 샀어요?

      B: 산 게 아니고 언니한테 _____.

      A: 언니가 동생한테 가방을 _____?

G7.3   ~어/아 있다 'In the state of being . . .'

Examples

(1)   손님: 이 사과 얼마해요?
      주인: 한 상자에 10,000원이에요.
      손님: 한 상자에 몇 개나 들**어 있어요**?   About how many are in a box?

      주인: 스무 개 들**어 있어요**.   Twenty are in (there).

(2)   지연: 어휴, 배 아파. 소연아, 약 있니?
      소연: 어떡하지? 약이 없는데.
      지연: 약국 아직 열**려 있**을까?
      소연: 지금 11시 반이니까 아직   Since it's 11:30 now,
           열**려 있**을 거야.   it'll still be open.
           내가 빨리 가서 사 올게.

(3)   손님: 와, 싱싱한 과일이 아주 많이   Wow! So many fresh
           나**와 있**네요!   fruits are out here.
      주인: 네, 나온 지 얼마 안 돼요.
           좀 보실래요?
      손님: 사과하고 배 좀 보여 주세요.

(4)   우진: 동수 씨, 요즘 성희 왜 안 보여요?
      동수: 모르셨어요?
           성희 씨 지금 영어 공부하러 미국에 **가 있어요**.

Notes

1. ~어/아 있다 expresses that a person or object is in a persistent state, typically resulting from a previous action designated by the verb. For example, apples being in a box in (1) is the result of someone having put

them in the box. Similarly, in (4), 성희's being in the United States is the result of her having gone to the States. It should be noted, however, that what is focused with ~어/아 있다 is the current state of affairs, not the previous action that caused it.

2. The ~어/아 variation is the same as that of ~어요/아요, ~어서/아서, ~었/았, etc.

3. ~어/아 있다 is contrasted with ~고 있다, which expresses that a person or object is in a dynamic (progressive) process.

마이클이 의자에 앉고 있다.   마이클이 의자에 앉아 있다.

Exercise

Describe the given pictures using ~어/아 있다.

(1)   제임스가 의자에 _____

(2)   스티브는 _____

(3) 분이 _____

(4) 문이 _____

(5) 영어로 _____

(6) 리사가 침대에 _____
(눕다 'to lie down')

Conversation 2 │ 여기 뭐 사러 왔어?

(우진은 슈퍼에서 우연히 수빈을 만났다.)

우진: 수빈아, 뭐 사러 왔어?

수빈: 응, 우유하고 빵하고 계란 좀 사러 왔어.
           너도 여기 자주 오니?

우진: 아니, 보통은 마트에 가는데 오늘 좀
           급해 가지고[G7.4] 몇 가지만 좀 사려고.

수빈: 응. 뭐 사야 되는데?

우진: 치약이랑 칫솔이랑 비누 좀 사야 돼.
           근데, 잡채 만드는 데에[G7.5] 야채가 뭐뭐
           들어가?

수빈: 보통 양파하고 당근, 시금치를 넣는데
           나는 그냥 냉장고 열어 보고 있는 야채
           다 집어 넣어.

우진: 그래, 이번 주말에 만들어 봐야겠다.

COMPREHENSION QUESTIONS

1. 수빈이는 슈퍼에서 무엇을 사려고 합니까?
2. 우진이는 슈퍼에서 무엇을 사려고 합니까?
3. 잡채에는 무엇이 들어갑니까?

NEW WORDS

NOUN		화장품	cosmetics
계란	egg	휴지	toilet paper
고기	meat	**VERB**	
당근	carrot	끓이다	to boil
마트	mart	넣다	to put in
비누	soap	들르다	to stop by
빵	bread	싸우다	to fight
시금치	spinach	울다	to cry
시장	market	웃다	to laugh
야채	vegetable	원하다	to wish
양파	onion	집어넣다	to put something in
우유	milk	**ADJECTIVE**	
잡채	*japchae*	다양하다	to be diverse
치약	toothpaste	**SUFFIX**	
칫솔	tooth-brush	~(으)ㄴ/는 데에	in/for ~ing
파	scallion	~어/아 가지고	because; by doing
호박	pumpkin, squash		

NEW EXPRESSIONS

1. Several terms are used for stores where you can buy your daily groceries and other items, depending on the size of the store as well as the types of products they carry.

편의점	convenience store (e.g., 7-Eleven)
슈퍼마켓 (슈퍼)	market (e.g., small stores)
마트	mart (e.g., Walmart)

2. When a question includes more than one item to be taken as an answer, speakers duplicate some question words such as 뭐뭐, 어디어디, 누구누구.

> A: 파티에 누구누구 초대했어요?
> B: 마크랑 제니랑 린다를 초대했어요.
>
> A: 마트에서 뭐뭐 살 거예요?
> B: 빵이랑 우유랑 과일을 사야 돼요.

G7.4   ~어/아 가지고 'because, since'; 'by doing/being'

Examples

[Expressing a causal relation]

(1)   소연: 장 보러 자주 가?
       성희: 우리 냉장고가 작**아 가지고**,   Because our refrigerator is
              일주일에 두 번은 봐야 돼.   small, I have to come here
                                           twice a week.

(2)   A: 보통 과일은 어디에서 사 먹어요?
       B: 시장이 너무 멀**어 가지고** 편의점에서 사요.

(3)   A: 보통 어디서 장을 보세요?
       B: 물건이 싸고 다양**해 가지고** 마트에 자주 가는 편이에요.

[Expressing two sequential events]

(4)   동수: 고기는 누가 살 거예요?
       우진: 내가 **사 가지고** 갈게요.   I'll buy them (and take
                                            them to the party).

(5)   선생님:오늘 숙제 다 **해 가지고** 왔어요?
       민지: 숙제 있었어요? 저는 몰랐어요.

(6)   동수: 방학 동안 뭐 했어요?
      우진: 아르바이트 **해 가지고** 컴퓨터를 새로 샀어요.

Notes

1. 가지다 literally means 'to have/possess', but is idiomatized as 'with' or 'by' in ~어/아 가지고. ~어/아 가지고 is similar in usage to ~어/아서 in that both express two sequential events as in (1–3), and sometimes also a causal relation as in (4–6), where the first event triggers the second.

2. These functions of ~어/아 가지고 are similar to those of ~어서/아서. In fact it seems that in many instances, ~어 가지고 is replacing ~어서 in spoken language, limiting the use of ~어서/아서 to those cases where the two events conjoined are closely tied together. In the following examples, for instance, ~이시/아서 cannot be replaced with ~어/아 가지고.

늦어서 미안합니다.
머리가 아파서 먼저 집에 갈게요.
걸어서 학교에 가요.
집에 갈 때 빵집에 들러서 가세요.

A: 어제 왜 병원에 갔어요?
B: 배가 아파서 갔어요.

3. In speech, ~어/아 가지고 is pronounced as [어/아 가지구] or contracted to ~어/아 갖고, which is pronounced as [어/아 가꼬], [어/아 가꾸] or [어/아 각꾸].

Exercises

1. Using ~어/아 가지고, make up a dialogue according to the given context.

(1)   A: 제니가 왜 울어요?
      B: <u>동생하고 싸워 가지고</u> 우는 것 같아요.

(2)   A: 어, 학교에 안 갔어요?
      B: _____ 못 일어나겠어요.

(3)   A: 사는 동네 어때요?

       B: 이사온 지 _____ 잘 모르겠어요.
              1주일 전에 이사왔거든요.

(4)   A: 새로 이사간 아파트 어때요?

       B: _____ 조금 불편해요.
              시장이 조금 더 가까이 있으면 좋겠어요.

(5)   A: 어제 파티에 왜 안 왔어요?

       B: 미안해요. _____ 못 갔어요.

(6)   A: 어디 가세요?

       B: 휴지가 _____ 마트에 사러
              가는 길이에요.

2.   Say the following sentences using ~어/아 가지고.

       (1)   Please do your homework and bring it the day after
              tomorrow.
       (2)   Having studied economics in the United States, my older
              brother returned to Korea.
       (3)   Having not studied hard, my younger brother failed the
              college entrance exam.

3.   Answer the following questions using ~어/아 가지고.

       (1)   A: 이번 시험 잘 봤어?
              B: _____.
       (2)   A: 어젯밤에 왜 전화했어?
              B: _____.
       (3)   A: 김 선생님은 왜 하루 종일 웃으세요?
              B: _____.
       (4)   A: 한국어를 왜 배우세요?
              B: _____.

G7.5   ~는 데(에) 'in/for ~ing . . .'

Examples

(1)   성희: 아주머니, 된장찌개 끓이**는 데(에)** 뭐가 들어가죠?   What goes in in making 된장찌개?

   주인: 두부하고 호박을 넣고, 파도 필요해요.

(2)   소연: 현대 소나타 하루 빌리**는 데(에)** 얼마예요?   How much is it for renting a Hyundai Sonata for one day?

   직원: 하루 삼만 원이에요.

(3)   주인: 지내**는 데(에)** 뭐 불편한 거 없어요?
   마크: 네, 없어요. 시장도 가깝고 교통도 편하고 다 좋아요. 전에는 장 보**는 데(에)** 세 시간이 걸렸는데, 지금은 30분이면 돼요.

(4)   A: 시장이 여기서 멀어요?
   B: 아니요, 지하철 역까지 걸어 가**는 데에**만 한 20분 걸리고, 지하철만 타면 금방 가요.

Notes

1. 데 literally means a 'place', but 데 in ~는 데(에) refers to a place in a more abstract sense, that is, an activity or a situation. It can be best translated as 'in ~ing' or 'for ~ing'.

2. It should be noted that ~는 데 should be written with a space between 는 and 데, distinguished from ~는데, which refers to background circumstances.

Exercise

Find out from the given context what situation the people are up to, and make up a dialogue using ~는 데(에).

(1)   A: <u>된장찌개 끓이는 데에</u> 뭐뭐 넣어요?

       B: 두부하고 호박을 넣고, 파도 넣어야 해요.

(2)   A: _____?

       B: 하루 삼만 원이에요. 현대 소나타는 좀 비싸거든요.

             요즘은 엘란트라도 많이 빌리는데 지금은 없어요.

(3)   [A is going to a dance party.]

       A: _____ 어떤 옷이 어울려요?

       B: 검정색이나 하늘색이 어때요?

(4)   A: 아, 배 아파. 약 있으면 좀 줄래?

       B: 여기 있어.

       A: 이거 말고 다른 거 없어?

       B: 왜? _____는 이 약이 제일 좋아.

(5)   [스티브 moved in just a few days ago.]

       하숙집 주인: _____ 불편한 거 없어요?

       스티브: 네, 없어요. 다 좋아요.

Narration   동네 시장

우진이는 한 달 전에 지금 사는 원룸으로 이사를 왔다.
기숙사에서는 장 보는 것이 불편했는데 지금 사는
집에서는 큰 길을 건너면 바로 그 앞에 시장이 있어서
편하다. 시장에는 큰 슈퍼마켓, 과일 가게, 야채 가게,
생선 가게, 정육점, 빵집도 있고, 옷 가게, 신발 가게,
화장품 가게, 약국 등이 있어서 필요한 물건들을 쉽게
살 수 있다. 물건 값도 백화점보다 싼 편이다. 물건을
많이 사면 배달도 해 주기 때문에 아주 편리하다. 특히,
동네 시장에는 편의점도 있는데 24시간 열려 있어서
늦은 시간에도 원하는 물건을 살 수 있다.

정육점 butcher's shop

COMPREHENSION QUESTIONS

1. 우진이는 언제 지금 사는 아파트로 이사왔습니까?
2. 지금 사는 아파트에서 시장에 가려면 어떻게 합니까?
3. 슈퍼마켓은 왜 편리합니까?
4. 어디서 배달을 해 줍니까?

CULTURE

택배

물건을 배달할 때 요즘 한국 사람들이 가장 많이 사용하는 서비스는
택배다. 택배로 물건을 받기도 하고 보내기도 한다. 택배로 물건을 받을
때는 택배 기사에게 사인을
해 주어야 한다.

　　　　인터넷 쇼핑을 할
때도 택배로 물건을 받는다.
백화점에서 옷이나 신발을
사고 나서 수선을 했을 때
택배로 집에 배달이 된다.
추석이나 설날, 크리스마스
같은 때에는 많은 사람들이 택배 서비스를 사용하기 때문에 배달 시간이
다른 때보다 좀 더 오래 걸릴 수 있지만, 보통 때는 하루나 이틀이면
원하는 곳으로 물건들을 배달 시킬 수 있다.

무게	weight	원하다	to want
물품	articles, goods	택배	delivery service
사인	sign	회사	company
수선	alteration		

USAGE

1. Talking about food and making a shopping list

Examples

(1)　　(성희 and 소연 run into each other at a supermarket.)
　　　성희: 소연아, 여기 웬일이니? 뭐 사러 왔니?
　　　소연: 응, 휴지도 사고 또 오렌지 주스랑 과일 좀 사러 왔어.
　　　　　　너도 장 보러 왔니?
　　　성희: 응, 난 집에서 밥을 해 먹으니까 살 게 많아.
　　　소연: 오늘 저녁 메뉴가 뭔데?
　　　성희: 된장찌개 끓이려고. 감자 (potatoes), 호박, 양파, 마늘
　　　　　　(garlic), 콩나물 (bean sprouts) 샀어.
　　　　　　아, 참. 시금치하고 계란도 사야 되는데.
　　　소연: 그럼, 어서 장 봐.
　　　성희: 그래, 또 보자. 잘 가.

(2)　　주인: 어서 오세요. 뭘 드릴까요?
　　　성희: 감자하고 파 좀 주세요.
　　　주인: 감자는 몇 개 드릴까요?
　　　성희: 4개 주세요. 파는 두 단 주세요.
　　　　　　참, 그리고 콩나물도 한 봉지 주세요.

Locating items at a supermarket

　　　　　_____이/가 어디 있어요?

Inquiring about the price of items at a grocery store.

　　　오렌지 하나에 얼마예요?
　　　사과 한 상자에 얼마예요?

[Exercise 1] Practice the above conversation (1) and make a shopping list
for 성희 and 소연.

소연's shopping list   성희's shopping list

_____   _____
_____   _____
_____   _____
_____   _____

Read your list to your class.

[Exercise 2] Look at 우진's shopping list below and role-play a conversation between 우진 and the grocer.

시장 볼 것들 (shopping list)
      소고기 500그램
      감자 4 개
      콩나물 1 봉지
      사과 한 상자
      호박 큰 것 두 개
      파 두 단
      과일
      고추장 작은 것 하나

[Exercise 3] Write a grocery list for yourself.

[Exercise 4] Exchange the following information with a classmate.

      (1)   시장 보러 얼마나 자주 가세요?
      (2)   어느 슈퍼마켓에 잘 가세요?
      (3)   생선(fish)을 좋아하세요, 고기를 좋아하세요?
      (4)   야채 많이 드세요?
      (5)   무슨 과일을 제일 좋아하세요?
      (6)   저녁에 보통 뭐 먹어요?

[Exercise 5] Role-play the following situations.

      (1)   Your roommate is going to go to the Korean market in
               town. Ask him or her to buy some Korean food for you.

(2)   You are at the Korean supermarket, and you want to know the price of a product and where to find it at the market.

2. Making recipes

Examples

(1)   [불고기 샌드위치 만들기]

재료: 빵, 쇠고기, 간장 1큰술, 설탕 1/2큰술, 참기름 1/2작은술
파, 마늘 1작은술, 후추 약간, 상추 2장, 토마토 2개

만드는 법:

① 소고기를 얇게 썰어 간장, 설탕, 참기름, 파, 마늘, 후추를
넣어 양념한다.
② 팬을 뜨겁게 달구어 양념한 불고기를 넣어 볶는다.
③ 상추는 씻는다.
④ 토마토는 얇게 썰어 둔다.
⑤ 빵 위에 상추와 토마토를 깔고 그 위에 불고기를 얹는다.

(2)   [라면 만들기]

① 끓는 물 (3컵 정도)에 면과 스프를 넣고 4-5 분간 더
끓이면 맛있는 라면이 됩니다.
② 식성에 따라 김치, 계란, 파 등을 넣어 드시면 더 맛이
좋습니다.

Useful words: 소고기 beef, 간장 soy sauce, 설탕 sugar, 참기름 sesame oil, 파 green onions, 마늘 garlic, 후추 black pepper, 상추 lettuce, 토마토 tomatoes, 큰술 tablespoon, 만드는 법 recipe, 얇게 썰다 thin slice, 양념하다 to season, 팬 pan, 달구다 to heat, 볶다 to stir-fry, 씻다 to wash, 두다 to put aside, 깔다 to spread, 얹다 to put on top , 끓다 to boil, 면 noodles, 스프 soup base, 식성 appetite, 에 따라 according to

[Exercise 1] Converse with your partner about the recipe above.

> Example
> A: 불고기 만드는 데에 무슨 재료가 필요해요?
> B: 쇠고기, 간장, 설탕, 참기름, 파, 마늘, 후추가 필요해요.

[Exercise 2] Describe your favorite recipe in Korean.

3. Expressing hesitation

Examples

> (At a clothing store)
> 점원: 손님, 이게 요새 유행하는 스타일이에요.
>   이걸 한번 입어 보세요.
> 손님: 글쎄요. (implying "I am not quite comfortable with this
>   style.")
>   이런 스타일은 한번도 안 입어 봐서 어떨지 모르겠어요.
> 점원: 그럼, 이런 스타일은 어떠세요?
> 손님: 색깔이 좀 . . . (expressing some reservation about the color)

You can express your reservations in various contexts. Hesitation devices give you time to think and to respond in a polite manner. There are various linguistic devices in Korean to express one's reservations. For example,

저어/저 (with a hesitant tone)	uh, um
저기요	Excuse me.
음	uh, um
글쎄요	Well, I am not quite sure.
사실은요	in fact, to tell you the truth
있잖아요.	you know

You can use hesitation devices in the following situations.

> (1)   To get the attention of a stranger
>   저어 (as a conversation opener)
>   실례합니다. 말씀 좀 묻겠습니다.

(2)   To call a customer
저기요 'Excuse me.'
손님, 거스름돈 받아 가셔야지요.

(3)   To make a request or ask a favor
저 (with a hesitant tone), 미안하지만, 부탁이 하나
있는데요.

(4)   When expressing one's opinion
Another way of expressing one's reservation is to use
incomplete sentences as in the model dialogue in the box
above (e.g., 색깔이 좀 . . .).

[Exercise] Role-play the following situations. Use some of the hesitation
devices listed above. Don't use silence to express hesitation.

(1)   You're calling out to a stranger who has forgotten her
purse on a chair.
(2)   You want to ask a stranger on the street for directions to
the nearest post office.
(3)   You visit your Korean professor's office without an
appointment and find that she or he is busy.

Lesson 7. At a store

CONVERSATION 1: How much is one box of apples?

(Woojin went to the fruit store in his neighborhood to buy fruits.)

Woojin:	How are you, ma'am?
Owner:	Oh, long time no see. Have you been somewhere all this time?
Woojin:	Yes, I was at my home in the United States during the vacation.
Owner:	You were?
Woojin:	Wow! These fruits look delicious. Which fruit sells well these days?
Owner:	Apples and pears tend to sell well.
Woojin:	How much is one box of apples?
Owner:	It is 20,000 won.
Woojin:	How many apples are there in one box?
Owner:	There are ten.
Woojin:	These tangerines also look delicious. How much are the tangerines?
Owner:	It is 1,000 won for three.
Woojin:	Then, please give me 3,000 won's worth.

CONVERSATION 2: What did you come here to buy?

(Woojin met Soobin at the market by chance.)

Woojin:	Soobin, what did you come to buy?
Soobin:	Well, I'm going to buy milk, bread, and eggs. Do you come here often?
Woojin:	No, usually I go to the big mart. However, I'm here because I urgently need to buy a few things.
Soobin:	I see. What do you have to buy?
Woojin:	I am going to buy toothpaste, a tooth brush, and soap. By the way, what vegetables do I need for making *japchae*?
Soobin:	They usually put in onions, carrots, and spinach, but I just open the refrigerator and put in any vegetables that I have.
Woojin:	Okay. I will try making it this weekend.

NARRATION: Market in the neighborhood

Woojin moved into a studio one month ago, which is where he now lives. It used to be inconvenient to go grocery shopping when he lived at the dormitory, but now, grocery shopping is convenient because there is a market directly across the big road from where he lives. It is easy to buy necessary items at the marketplace because there is a big supermarket, fruit store, vegetable store, fish store, butcher, and bakery as well as a clothing store, shoe store, cosmetics store, pharmacy, and so on. The prices are on the cheap side when compared to those of department stores. It is very convenient because the shops have delivery service for those who buy a lot. Especially convenient is the convenience store at the marketplace in the neighborhood. He can buy items at any time there because it is open twenty-four hours a day.

CULTURE: 택배

택배 is the most popular service when Korean people deliver articles these days. People receive and send articles using 택배. When you receive an article by 택배, you need to sign for it.

You receive items that you shopped for online by 택배. Clothes or shoes that you bought at the department store are delivered to your house through 택배 after alteration. Usually you can expect delivery in one or two days except on days like Thanksgiving or New Year's Day or Christmas when many people use 택배 service and delivery takes a little longer than usual.

Grammar Index

Item	Meaning	Lesson
~(으)ㄴ/는지 알다/모르다	to know/not know whether	Lesson 5 C1
~(으)니까	expresses reason	Lesson 3 C2
~(으)려고 하다	intend to	Lesson 2 C1
~(으)려면	if . . . intends to	Lesson 4 C2
~(으)면 되다	all one needs is	Lesson 3 C1
~(으)면 좋겠다	I wish	Lesson 1 C2
~잖아요	you know	Lesson 1 C1

Korean - English Glossary

1학년	freshman	개	1. dog;
2학년	sophomore		2. item (counter)
3학년	junior	개월	month
4학년	senior	거	thing (contraction of 것)
가	subject particle		
가게	store	거기	there
가격	price	거리	1. distance;
가구	furniture		2. street, avenue
가구점	furniture store	거스름돈	change (money)
가깝다	to be close, near	거실	living room
가끔	sometimes	거의	almost
가다	to go	걱정	worry, concern
가르치다	to teach	걱정하다	to worry
가방	bag	건강하다	to be healthy
가볍다	to be light	건너다	to cross
가수	singer	건너편	the other side
가운데	the middle, the center	건물	building
가위, 바위, 보	rock-paper-scissors	건조하다	to be dry
가을	autumn, fall	건축물	building, structure
가장	the most	건축학	architecture
가져가다	to take, carry	걷다	to walk
가족	family	걸다	to call
각	each	걸리다	to take [time]
간장	soy sauce	걸어가다	to go on foot
간판	store signs	걸어다니다	to walk around
갈비	*kalbi* (spareribs)	걸어오다	to come on foot
갈아 입다	to change (clothes)	검정 색	black
갈아 타다	to change (vehicles)	것	thing (=거)
감기에 걸리다	to have/catch a cold	게임	game
감사하다	to be thankful	겨울	winter
감자	potato	결혼	marriage
갑자기	suddenly	결혼식	wedding
값	price	결혼하다	to get married
강원	Gangwon region	경기	match, game
갖고 가다	to take	경우	case
갖고 다니다	to carry around	경제학	economics
갖고 오다	to bring	경주	Gyeongju
갖다 놓다	to bring and put down somewhere	경찰	police
갖다	to bring/take	경찰서	police station
드리다*hum.*	something to someone	경치	scenery, view
갖다 주다*plain*	to bring/take something to someone	경험	experience
		계단	stairs
		계란	egg
같이	together	계산서	check

계속	continuously	교실	classroom
계속되다	to continue	교육학	education
계시다 *hon.*	to be (existence), stay	교통	traffic
계절	season	교통 표지판	traffic sign
계좌	account	교통카드	transportation card
계획	plan	교회	church
계획하다	to plan	구경	sightseeing
고기	meat	구경하다	to look around; to
고등학교	high school		sightsee
고등학생	high school student	구두	dress shoes
고르다	to choose, select	구두 시험	oral exam
고맙다	to be thankful	구름	cloud
고생	hardship	구름이 끼다	to get cloudy
고생하다	to have a difficult time	구하다	to search for
고속도로	highway, freeway	국경일	national holidays
고장	breakdown	국내선	domestic flight
고장나다	to break down	국제선	international flight
고추장	red-pepper paste	국제 전화	international call
고층빌딩	high-rise building	군데	place, spot
고향	hometown	굽	heel
곧	right away, soon	권	volume (counter)
골동품	antique	귀걸이	earring
골프	golf	귤	tangerine
곳	place	그	that
공	0 (zero: for phone #)	그냥	just, without any
공기	air		special reason
공부	study	그동안	meantime
공부방	study room	그래서	so, therefore
공부하다	to study	그램	gram
공사	construction	그러면	then, in that case
공예품	craftwork	그런데	1. but, however;
공원	park		2. by the way
공장	factory	그럼	(if so) then
공포 영화	horror movie	그렇다	to be so
공항	airport	그렇지만	but, however
과	1. lesson, chapter;	그릇	dish
	2. and (joins nouns)	그리고	and
과목	course, subject	그리다	to draw
과일	fruit	그림	picture, painting
과자	cracker	그립다	to miss, long for
과학	science	그만	without doing
관악산	Gwanak Mountain		anything further
괜찮다	to be all right, okay	극장	movie theater
굉장히	very much	근처	nearby, vicinity
교과서	textbook	글쎄요	Well; It's hard to say
교복	school uniform	금반지	gold ring
교수님	professor	금방	soon

금요일	Friday
기계 공학	mechanical engineering
기다려지다	to be wished
기다리다	to wait
기분	feeling
기쁘다	to be joyful, glad
기사	driver
기숙사	dormitory
기억	memory
기억하다	to remember
기온	temperature
기원전	B.C.
기차	train
기타	guitar
길	1. street, road ; 2. way
길다	to be long
김밥	*kimbap*
김치	kimchi
까만색	black (=까망)
까맣다	to be black
까지	1. up to (location); 2. to/until/through (time); 3. including
깎다	to cut down
깔다	to spread
깨끗하다	to be clean
깨지다	to break
께*hon.*	to (a person)
께서*hon.*	subject particle (=이/가 *plain*)
꼭	surely, certainly
꽃	flower
꽃집	flower shop
꿈(을) 꾸다	to dream a dream
끓이다	to boil
끝나다	to be over, finished
끼다	to be foggy
끼다	to wear (glasses, gloves, rings)
나*plain*	I (=저*hum.*)
나가다	to go out
나다	happen, break out
나라	country
나쁘다	to be bad

나오다	to come out
나이	age
나이가 들다	to gain age
나중에	later
나타내다	to show, represent
나흘	four days
난방	heating
날	day
날마다	every day
날씨	weather
날씬하다	to be thin
날짜	date
남	south
남기다	to leave (a message)
남다	to remain
남동생	younger brother
남미	South America
남부	southern
남산	Nam Mountain
남색	navy blue, indigo
남아있다	to remain
남자	man
낮	daytime
낮다	to be low
낮아지다	to get lower
내*plain*	my (=제*hum.*)
내년	next year
내다	1. to pay (money); 2. to turn in (homework)
내려가다	to go down
내리다	to get off
내일	tomorrow
냉면	*naengmyŏn* (cold buckwheat noodles)
냉장고	refrigerator
너	you *plain*
너무	too much
넓다	to be spacious, wide
넘어지다	to fall (down)
넣다	to put in
네	1. yes; 2. I see; 3. okay
네거리	intersection
넥타이	necktie
년	year (counter)

노란색	yellow
노랗다	to be yellow
노래	song
노래 부르다	to sing
노래하다	to sing
노래방	karaoke room
녹차	green tea
놀다	to play; to not work
놀라다	to be surprised
농구	basketball
농구하다	to play basketball
농구 시합	basketball game
농사	farming
높다	to be high
놓아 주다	to put something down for someone
누가	1. who (누구+가); 2. someone
누구	1. who; 2. someone
누나	the older sister of a male
눈(이) 오다	to snow
눈	1. eyes; 2. snow
눕다	to lie down
뉴스	news
뉴욕	New York
는	topic particle ('as for')
늘다	to improve
늦게	late
늦다	to be late
늦잠	oversleep
다	all
다녀 오다	to go and get back
다니다	1. to attend; 2. to get around
다르다	to be different
다보탑	Dabo Tower
다소	more or less; to some degree
다시	again
다양하다	to be diverse
다음	next, following
다음부터(는)	from next time
다치다	to hurt
단	bundle; bunch

단어	vocabulary
단정하다	to be neat
단풍	fall foliage
닫다	to close
닫히다	to be closed
달	1. month (counter); 2. moon
달구다	to heat
달다	to be sweet
달러	dollar (=불)
달력	calendar
닮다	to resemble
담배	cigarette
답	answer
답장	reply
답장하다	to reply
당근	carrot
대답	answer
대답하다	to answer
대중	the public
대체로	generally, mostly
대충	roughly
대통령	president
대통령 선거	presidential election
대학	college, university
대학교	college, university
대학생	college student
대학원	graduate school
대학원생	graduate student
대한항공	Korean Air
대해서	about
댁*hon.*	home, house (=집*plain*)
더	more
더럽다	to be dirty
덜	less
덥다	to be hot
덮다	to close, cover
데	place
데이트	a date
데이트하다	to date
도	1. also, too; 2. degree
도둑	thief
도서관	library
도시	city
도와 드리다*hon.*	to help
도와 주다*plain*	to help

도움	help	들어오다	to come in
도착하다	to arrive	들어있다	to contain
도쿄	Tokyo	등	et cetera
독방	single room	등기	registered (mail)
독서	reading	등산	hiking
독서하다	to read	등산객	mountain climber
돈	money	등산하다	to hike
돈을 내다	to pay	따님hon.	daughter
돈을 벌다	to earn money	따뜻하다	to be warm
돈이 들다	to cost money	따라하다	to repeat after
돌	the first birthday	딸	daughter
돌다	to turn	때	time
돌려 드리다hum.	to return (something to someone)	때문에	because of
		떠나다	to leave
돌려 주다plain	to return (something to someone)	또	and, also, too
		똑같다	to be identical
돌아가다	to return (to)	똑바로	straight, upright
돌아가시다hon.	to pass away	뚱뚱하디	to be fat
돌아오다	to return, come back	뛰다	to run
돕다	to help	뜨겁다	to be hot
동	east	뜨다	to rise; to come up
동남아	Southeast Asia	뜻하다	to mean, signify
동네	neighborhood	라디오	radio
동대문시장	Dongdaemun Market	라면	instant noodles (ramen)
동물원	zoo		
동부	East Coast	라운지	lounge
동생	younger sibling	램프	lamp
동안	during	랩	lab
동양학	Asian studies	러시아	Russia
되다	1. to become; 2. get, turn into; 3. to function, work	런던	London
		로스앤젤레스	Los Angeles (L.A.)
		록	rock music
된장찌개	soybean-paste stew	룸메이트	roommate
두	two (with counter)	를	object particle
두 번째	the second	마늘	garlic
두껍다	to be thick	마당	yard
두부	tofu	마르다	to be skinny
둘	two	마리	animal (counter)
뒤	the back, behind	마시다	to drink
드라마	drama	마을 버스	town shuttle bus
드럼	drum	마음	mind, heart
드리다hum.	to give (=주다plain)	마음에 들다	to be to one's liking
드시다hon.	to eat (=먹다plain)	마중 나가다	to go out to greet someone
들다	1. to listen; 2. to take a course		
		마중 나오다	to come out to greet someone
들	plural particle		
들르다	to stop by	마침	just, just in time
들어가다	to enter	마켓	market

마트	mart	몇	how many, what (with a counter)
막내	youngest child		
막히다	to be blocked, congested	모두	all
		모레	the day after tomorrow
만	only		
만나다	to meet	모르다	to not know, be unaware of
만드는 법	recipe		
만들다	to make	모양	shape
만화방	comic book rental store	모으다	to collect
		모이다	to gather
만화책	comic book	모자	cap, hat
많다	to be many, much	모자라다	to lack
많이	much, many	모텔	motel
말	speech, words	목(이) 마르다	to be thirsty
말고	not N1 but N2	목걸이	necklace
말씀*hon.*	speech, words (=말 *plain*)	목도리	muffler, scarf
		목소리	voice
말하다	to speak	목요일	Thursday
맑다	to be clear	목욕	bath
맛보다	to taste	목욕하다	to bathe
맛없다	to be tasteless, not delicious	몸	body
		몸조리	care of health
맛있다	to be delicious	못	cannot
맞다	1. to fit; 2. to be correct	못생기다	to be ugly
		무겁다	to be heavy
매년	every year	무게	weight
매다	to tie	무덥다	to be hot and humid
매달	every month	무료	free of charge
매일	every day	무섭다	to be scary; scared
매주	every week	무슨	1. what, what kind of; 2. some kind of
매표소	ticket office		
맵다	to be spicy	무엇	what (=뭐)
머리	1. head; 2. hair	무척	very much
		문	door
먹거리	things to eat	문제	problem
먹다	to eat	문학	literature
먼저	first, beforehand	문화	culture
멀다	to be far	묻다	to ask
멋있다	to be stylish, attractive	물	water
메뉴	menu	물가	cost of living
메시지	message	물건	merchandise, stuff
멕시코	Mexico	물다	to bite
며칠	1. what date; 2. a few days	물리다	to be bitten
		물리학	physics
면	noodles	물어보다	to inquire
명	people (counter)	물품	articles, goods
명절	traditional holidays		

뭐	1. what (=무엇);	배(가) 부르다	to have a full stomach
	2. something	배달	delivery
미국	the United States	배달하다	to deliver
미안하다	to be sorry	배우다	to learn
미용실	beauty salon	배터리	battery
미터기	meter	백만	million
밑	the bottom, below	백화점	department store
바겐 세일	bargain sale	밴쿠버	Vancouver
바꾸다	to change, switch	버스	bus
바뀌다	to be changed	번	1. number (counter);
바다	sea		2. number of times
바닥	floor		(e.g., 한 번)
바닷가	beach	번째	ordinal numbers
바람	wind	번호	number
바로	directly	벌	a pair of (counter)
바빠지다	to get busier	벌다	to earn (money)
바쁘다	to be busy	벌써	already
바이올린	violin	법학	law
바지	pants	벗다	to take off, undress
박물관	museum	별	star
박스	box	별로	not really/particularly
밖	outside	병원	hospital
밖에	nothing but, only	보내다	1. to spend time;
반	1. class;		2. to send
	2. half	보다	to see, look, watch
반갑다	to be glad	보다	than
반값	half price	보스톤	Boston
반드시	surely, certainly	보이다	to be seen, visible
반바지	shorts	보통	1. usually;
반지	ring		2. regular
반찬	side dishes	복	good fortune
받다	to receive	복도	aisle
발	foot	복습	review
발달	development	복잡하다	to be crowded
발달하다	to develop, grow	볶다	to stir-fry
발매기	vending machine	본인 확인	self-identification
밝다	to be bright	볼거리	things to watch
밤	night	볼링	bowling
밥	1. cooked rice;	볼펜	ballpoint pen
	2. meal	봄	spring
방	room	봉지	pack; bag
방금	a moment ago	봉투	envelope
방송국	broadcasting station	뵙다*hum.*	to see (=보다*plain*)
방학	school vacation	부르다 (노래)	to sing (a song)
배	1. stomach, abdomen;	부모님	parents
	2. pear	부엌	kitchen
배(가) 고프다	to be hungry	부자	a wealthy person

부족하다	to be insufficient	사랑	love
부치다	to mail (a letter, parcel)	사랑하다	to love
부탁하다	to ask a favor	사모님	teacher's wife
부터	from (time) . . .	사무실	office
북	north	사실	fact, truth
분	minute (counter)	사용하다	to use
분*hon.*	people (=명*plain*)	사우나	sauna
불	dollar (=달러)	사이	1. relationship;
불고기	*pulgogi* (roast meat)		2. between
불교	Buddhism	사이즈	size
불국사	Pulgugsa	사인	sign
불다	to blow	사전	dictionary
불편하다	to be uncomfortable,	사진	photo, picture
	inconvenient	사찰	temple
붙이다	to stick, affix	사투리	dialect
브로드웨이	Broadway theater	사회보장번호	Social Security
극장			number
블라우스	blouse	사흘	three days
비	rain	살	1. years old;
비(가) 오다	to rain		2. flesh, fat
비교적	relatively	살다	to live
비누	soap	삼	3
비빔밥	*pibimbap* (rice with	상	table
	vegetables and beef)	상가	shopping district
비슷하다	to be similar	상자	box
비싸다	to be expensive	상점	store
비자	visa	상추	lettuce
비행기	airplane	새	new
빌딩	building	새로	newly
빌려주다	to lend	새벽	dawn
빌리다	to borrow	새해	New Year
빠르다	to be fast	색	color (=색깔)
빨간색	red	샌드위치	sandwich
빨갛다	to be red	샌들	sandals
빨래하다	to do the laundry	생기다	to be formed
빨리	fast, quickly	생년월일	date of birth
빵	bread	생물학	biology
뺏기다	to be deprived of	생선	fish
사	4	생신*hon.*	birthday
사 먹다	to buy and eat	생일	birthday
사거리	intersection	생활	daily life, living
사고	accident	샤워	shower
사과	apple	샤워하다	to take a shower
사귀다	1. to make friends;	서	west
	2. to date	서기	A.D.
사다	to buy	서다	to stand
사람	person, people	서두르다	to hurry

서랍	drawer	쇼핑	shopping
서로	each other	쇼핑하다	to shop
서비스	service	수고하다	to put forth effort, take
서울	Seoul		trouble
서울대입구역	Seoul National	수도	capital city
	University Station	수선	alteration
서울타워	Seoul Tower	수업	course, class
서점	bookstore (=책방)	수영	swimming
석가탑	Seokga Tower	수영장	swimming pool
석굴암	Seokguram (stone	수영하다	to swim
	cave)	수요일	Wednesday
선물	present, gift	수저	spoon and chopsticks
선물하다	to give a present, gift	수프	soup
선생님	teacher	숙제	homework
설거지	dishwashing	숙제하다	to do homework
설거지하다	to wash dishes	순두부찌개	soft tofu stew
설악산	Seorak Mount	순가락	spoon
설탕	sugar	술	alcoholic beverage
섬	island	술집	pub, bar
섭씨	Celsius	숫자	number
성격	personality	쉬다	to rest
성별	sex, gender	쉽다	to be easy
성적	grade	슈퍼(마켓)	supermarket
성함 *hon.*	name (=이름 *plain*)	스릴러	thriller
세기	century	스시	sushi
세수하다	to wash one's face	스웨터	sweater
세우다	to stop, pull over	스키	ski
세일	sale	스키 타다	to ski
세탁기	washing machine	스타일	style
세탁소	laundry, cleaner's	스트레스	stress
세트	a set	스파게티	spaghetti
센트	cent	스페인	Spain
셔츠	shirt	스포츠	sports
소개	introduction	슬리퍼	slipper
소개하다	to introduce	슬프다	to be sad
소고기	beef	승차권	ride pass, ticket
소극적이다	to be passive	시	hour, o'clock
소리	sound, noise	시간	time, hour (duration)
소매	sleeve	시계	clock, watch
소방서	fire station	시금치	spinach
소설	novel	시끄럽다	to be noisy
소파	sofa	시내	downtown
소포	parcel, package	시다	to be sour
손	hand	시대	period
손(을) 씻다	to wash one's hands	시드니	Sydney
손님	guest, customer	시원하다	to be cool, refreshing
쇼	show	시원해지다	to become cooler

시작하다	to begin
시장	marketplace
시청	city hall
시청역	city hall station
시카고	Chicago
시키다	to order (food)
시합	game, match
시험	test, exam
식당	restaurant
식비	food expenses
식사	meal
식사하다	to have a meal
식성	appetite
식탁	dining table
신기하다	to be amazing
신나다	to be excited
신다	to wear (footwear)
신라	Silla
신문	newspaper
신문사	newspaper publisher
신발	shoes
신분증	identification card
신용 카드	credit card
신호등	traffic light
실	thread
실례하다	to be excused
싫다	to be undesirable
싫어하다	to dislike
심리학	psychology
심심하다	to be bored
싱겁다	to be bland
싶다	to want to
싸다	1. to be cheap;
	2. to wrap;
	3. to pack
싸우다	to fight
썰다	to slice
쓰다	1. to write;
	2. to use;
	3. to wear headgear;
	4. to be bitter
쓰이다	to be used
씨	attached to a person's name for courtesy
아	oh
아까	a while ago
아니다	to not be (negative equation)

아니요	no
아들	son
아래층	downstairs
아르바이트	part-time job
아름답다	to be beautiful
아마	probably, perhaps
아버지	father
아쉽다	to be sad, feel the lack of
아시아	Asia
아이	child
아이스크림	ice cream
아이스하키	ice hockey
아저씨	mister; a man of one's parents' age
아주	very, really
아주머니	middle-aged woman
아직	yet, still
아직도	yet, still
아침	1. breakfast; 2. morning
아파트	apartment
아프다	to be sick
악기	musical instrument
안	1. the inside; 2. do not
안개	fog
안경	eyeglasses
안녕하다	to be well
안녕히	in peace
안방	master bedroom
안부	regards
안전하다	to be safe
앉다	to sit
않다	to not be, to not do
알다	to know
알래스카	Alaska
알리다	to inform
알아듣다	to understand, recognize
알아보다	to find out, check out
앞	the front
액세서리	accessory
액션	action
야구	baseball
야구하다	to play baseball
야구장	baseball stadium

야외	the outside	얼음	ice
야채	vegetable	엄마	mom
약	1. approximately;	없다	1. to not be (existence);
	2. medicine		2. to not have
약국	drugstore	없어지다	to disappear
약도	map	에	1. in, at, on (static
약속	1. engagement;		location);
	2. promise		2. to (destination);
얇게	thinly		3. at, in, on (time);
얇다	to be thin		4. for, per
양념	condiment, seasoning	에 따라	according to
양념하다	to season	에서	1. in, at (dynamic
양력	solar calendar		location);
양말	socks, stockings		2. from (location);
양식	Western-style (food)		3. from (time)
양파	onion	에어컨	air conditioner
애기	talk, chat (=이야기)	엘리베이터	elevator
애기하다	to talk, chat	여권	passport
어	oh	여기	here
어느	which	여동생	younger sister
어둡다	to be dark	여러	many, several
어디	1. what place, where;	여름	summer
	2. somewhere	여보	honey, dear
어떤	which, what kind of	여보세요	hello (on the phone)
어떻게	how	여자	woman
어떻다	to be how	여자 친구	girlfriend
어렵다	to be difficult	여행	travel, trip
어른	adult, (one's) elders	여행사	travel agency
어리다	to be young	여행하다	to travel
어머	Oh! Oh my! Dear me!	역	station
어머니	mother	역사	history
어서	quick(ly)	연결	connection, link
어업	fishery	연결하다	to connect, link
어울리다	to match, suit	연구실	professor's office
어제	yesterday	연극	play, drama
어젯밤	last night	연락	contact
어치	worth, value	연락하다	to contact
언니	the older sister of a	연세 *hon.*	age (=나이 *plain*)
	female	연습	practice
언어학	linguistics	연습 문제	exercise
언제	1. when;	연습하다	to practice
	2. sometime	연주	musical performance
얹다	to put	연주하다	to perform on a
얼굴	face		musical instrument
얼다	to freeze	연필	pencil
얼마	how long/much	열다	to open
얼마나	how long/much	열리다	to be open

열쇠	key	외국인등록번호	Alien Registration
열심히	diligently		number
엽서	postcard	외롭다	to be lonely
영	0 (zero)	외식하다	to eat out
영국	the United Kingdom	외우다	to memorize
영서	Yeongseo region	왼쪽	left side
영수증	receipt	요금	fee, fare
영어	the English language	요리	cooking
영하	below the freezing	요리하다	to cook
	point	요새	these days
영화	movie	요즘	these days
옆	the side, beside	우리*plain*	we/us/our (=저희*hum.*)
예	yes, I see, okay (=네)	우산	umbrella
예를 들어	for example	우연히	by chance, accident
예쁘다	to be pretty	우유	milk
예술	art	우체국	post office
예약	reservation	우체부	postman
예약하다	to reserve	우체통	postbox
옛날	the old days	우편	mail service
오늘	today	우편 번호	postal code
오다	to come	우편 요금	postage
오래	long time	우표	stamp
오래간만	after a long time	운	luck, fortune
오랫동안	for a long time	운동	exercise
오른쪽	right side	운동장	playground
오빠	the older brother of a	운동하다	to exercise
	female	운동화	sports shoes, sneakers
오전	a.m.	운전	driving
오페라	opera	운전 면허	driver's license
오후	afternoon	운전하다	to drive
온돌	floor heating system	울다	to cry
올라가다	to go up	웃다	to laugh
올림	sincerely yours	원 (₩)	won (Korean
올림픽	Olympics		currency)
올해	this year	원룸	studio apartment
옮기다	to move, shift	원피스	(one-piece) dress
옷	clothes	원하다	to wish, want
옷가게	clothing store	월	month (counter)
옷장	wardrobe, closet	월드컵	World Cup
와	1. and (joins nouns);	월요일	Monday
	2. Wow!	웬일	what matter
와이셔츠	dress shirt	위	the top side, above
왕복	round-trip	위험하다	to be dangerous
왜	why	유난히	particularly
외국	foreign country	유니온 빌딩	Union Building
외국어	foreign language	유니폼	uniform
외국인	foreigner	유럽	Europe

유명하다	to be famous
유학생	student abroad
유행	fashion, trend
유행하다	to be in fashion
육개장	hot shredded-beef soup
으로	1. by means of; 2. toward, to; 3. item selected among many other options
은	topic particle ('as for')
은행	bank
을	object particle
음력	lunar calendar
음료수	beverage
음식	food
음식값	food cost
음식점	restaurant (=식당)
음악	music
음악회	concert
응	yeah
의	of
의사	doctor
의생활	clothing habits
의자	chair
이(를) 닦다	to brush one's teeth
이	1. 2; 2. subject particle; 3. this; 4. a suffix inserted after a Korean first name that ends in a consonant; 5. tooth
이거	this (=이것)
이기다	to win
이다	to be (equation)
이따가	a little later
이름	name
이메일	e-mail
이발소	barbershop
이번	this time
이사하다	to move
이스트 홀	East Hall
이야기	talk, chat (=얘기)
이야기하다	to talk (=얘기하다)
이용하다	to utilize

이젠	now (이제+는)
이쪽으로	this way + 으로
이태리	Italy
이틀	two days
이해하다	to understand
익숙하다	to be familiar
인구	population
인기	popularity
인도	sidewalk
인사	greeting
인사하다	to greet
인사동	Insadong
인사하다	to greet
인상적	memorable
인천	Incheon
인터넷	Internet
인터뷰	interview
일 인 분	one portion
일	1. 1; 2. day (counter); 3. work; 4. event
일기	journal
일기예보	weather forecast
일등석	first-class seat
일반석	economy-class seat
일본	Japan
일식	Japanese food
일어나다	to get up
일요일	Sunday
일찍	early
일하다	to work
읽다	to read
잃어버리다	to lose
입구	entrance
입다	to wear, put on (clothes)
있다	1. to be (existence); 2. to have
잊다	to forget
자다	to sleep
자동 응답기	answering machine
자동차	automobile
자라다	to grow up
자르다	to cut
자리	1. seat; 2. digit

자연	nature	적다	1. to be few, scarce;
자전거	bicycle		2. to write down
자주	often, frequently	적어도	at least
자취	living on one's own	적응	adaptation
자취하다	to live on one's own	적응하다	to adapt
자켓	jacket	전	before
작년	last year	전공	major
작다	to be small (in size)	전공하다	to major
잔	glass, cup	전기공학	electrical engineering
잔치	feast, party	전부	all together
잘	well	전세계	the whole world
잘라 드리다 *hum.*	to cut (something for someone)	전통	tradition
		전통 문화	traditional culture
잘라 주다 *plain*	to cut (something for someone)	전통 찻집	traditional teahouse
		전하다	to tell, convey
잘생기다	to be handsome	전화	telephone
잠	sleep	전화번호	telephone number
잠깐만	for a short time	전화비	telephone bill
잠실	Jamsil	전화하다	to make a telephone call
잠을 자다	to sleep		
잠이 들다	to fall asleep	절	Buddhist temple
잡다	to catch, grab	점심	lunch
잡지	magazine	점원	clerk, salesperson
잡채	*japchae*	점퍼	jumper/jacket
잡히다	to be caught	젓가락	chopsticks
장(을) 보다	to buy one's groceries	정가	regular price
장갑	gloves	정도	approximate
장거리 전화	long-distance call	정류장	(bus) stop
장롱	closet	정리	arrangement
장마	rainy season	정리하다	to arrange, organize
장소	place, location	정말	really
장학금	scholarship	정원	yard, garden
장화	boots	정육점	butcher shop
재미없다	to be uninteresting	정장	suit, formal dress
재미있다	to be interesting, fun	정치학	political science
재즈	jazz	정확하다	to be accurate
저	that (over there)	제 *hum.*	my (=내 *plain*)
저 *hum.*	I (=나 *plain*)	제과점	bakery
저기	over there	제일	first, most
저녁	1. evening; 2. dinner	제주도	Jeju Island
		조그맣다	to be small
저어	uh (expression of hesitation)	조금	a little (=좀)
		조심하다	to be careful
저절로	automatically	조용하다	to be quiet
저희 *hum.*	we/us/our (=우리 *plain*)	졸다	to doze off
적극적이다	to be positive	졸리다	to be sleepy
		졸업	graduation

졸업하다	to graduate	지금	now
졸업식	commencement	지나가다	to pass by
좀	a little (contraction of 조금)	지난	last, past
		지내다	to get along
좁다	to be narrow	지다	1. to lose;
종업원	employee		2. to go down (the Sun)
종이	paper		
좋다	to be good, nice	지도	map
좋아하다	to like	지방	region, district
좌석	seat	지역 번호	area code
죄송하다	to be sorry	지정하다	to appoint
주	week	지키다	to guard, protect
주다	to give	지하도	underpass
주로	mostly, mainly	지하 상가	underground market
주말	weekend	지하철	subway
주무시다hon.	to sleep (=자다plain)	직원	staff, employee
주문하다	to order	직장인	office worker
주민등록번호	Resident Registration number	직접	directly
		질문	question
주민등록증	Resident Registration card	짐	luggage, load
		집	home, house
주소	address	집어넣다	to put something in
주스	juice	짜다	to be salty
주유소	gas station	짜리	worth
주인	owner	짧다	to be short
주인공	main character	째	ordinal numbers
주차장	parking lot	쪽	1. page;
죽다	to die		2. side, direction
준비	preparation	쭉	straight
준비하다	to prepare	쯤	about, around
줄이다	to shorten	찍다	to take (a photo)
중간	the middle	찜질방	Korean dry sauna
중고 가구	used furniture	차	1. car;
중고품	used merchandise		2. tea
중국	China	차고	garage
중부 지방	the central districts	차다	to be cold
중식	Chinese food	차도	street, road
중심지	the pivot, center	차비	fare (bus, taxi)
중앙 우체국	Central Post Office	차차	gradually
중에서	between, among	착하다	to be good-natured, kindhearted
중요하다	to be important		
중학교	middle school	참	1. really, truly;
중학생	middle school student		2. by the way
즐겁다	to be joyful	참기름	sesame oil
즐기다	to enjoy	창가 좌석	window seat
지갑	wallet	찾다	1. to find, look for;
지겹다	to be boring		2. to withdraw(money)

책	book	컴퓨터	computer
책방	bookstore	컴퓨터 랩	computer lab
책상	desk	케이블카	cable car
책장	bookshelf, bookcase	케이크	cake
처음	the first time	켜다	to play (violin)
천천히	slow(ly)	켤레	pair (counter)
첫	first	코미디	comedy
청바지	blue jeans	코트	coat
청소	cleaning	콘서트	concert
청소기	vacuum cleaner	콘택트 렌즈	contact lens
청소하다	to clean	콜라	cola
초등학교	elementary school	콩나물	bean sprout
초등학생	elementary school student	쿠바	Cuba
		크게	loud(ly)
초록색	green	크다	to be big
최고	the highest	크리스마스	Christmas
최저	the lowest	큰술	tablespoon
추워지다	to get colder	큰아버지	uncle (father's older brother)
축구	soccer		
축구하다	to play soccer	클래스	class
축하하다	to congratulate	클래식	classical music
출구	exit	클럽	club
출발	departure	키	height
출발하다	to depart	키가 작다	to be short
춤	dance	키가 크다	to be tall
춤(을) 추다	to dance	타고 가다	to go riding
춥다	to be cold	타고 다니다	to come/go riding
취미	hobby	타고 오다	to come riding
층	floor, layer (counter)	타다	to get in/on, ride
치다	1. to play (tennis); 2. to play (piano, guitar)	타이레놀	Tylenol
		태권도	Taekwondo
		태어나다	to be born
치마	skirt	택배	delivery service
치약	toothpaste	택시	taxi
친구	friend	택시비	taxi fare
친절하다	to be kind, considerate	테니스	tennis
친하다	to be close (to)	테니스장	tennis court
칠판	blackboard	테이프	tape
침대	bed	텔레비전	television
침실	bedroom	토마토	tomato
칫솔	toothbrush	토요일	Saturday
카드	card	통화	phone call
카메라	camera	통화하다	to make a phone call
캐나다	Canada	트럭	truck
캠퍼스	campus	특별하다	to be special
커피	coffee	특히	particularly
커피숍	coffee shop, café		

틀다	to turn on, switch on, play (music)	하숙비	boarding expenses
		하숙집	boardinghouse
티셔츠	T-shirt	하얗다	to be white
티켓	ticket	하와이	Hawai'i
파	scallion	학교	school
파란색	blue	학기	academic term
파랗다	to be blue	학년	school year
파티	party	학비	tuition fees
팔다	to sell	학생	student
팔리다	to be sold	학생회관	student center
팬	pan	한	one (with counter)
펜	pen	한국	Korea
펴다	to open, unfold	한국말	the Korean language
편도	one-way trip	한국어	the Korean language
편리하다	to be convenient	한국학	Korean studies
편안하다	to be comfortable	한글	Korean alphabet
편의점	convenience store	한글날	Hangeul Day
편지	letter	한라산	Halla Mount
편하다	to be comfortable, convenient	한복	Korean traditional dress
포근하다	to be warm	한식	Korean food
포장	packing	한인타운	Korea town
폭포	waterfall	한테	to (a person or an animal)
표	ticket		
표지판	sign	한테서	from (a person or an animal)
풀다	to relieve		
풋볼	football	할머니	grandmother
프랑스	France	할아버지	grandfather
프로	program	할인	discount
피곤하다	to be tired	함께	together, along with
피다	to bloom	항공료	airfare
피시방	Internet café	항상	always
피아노	piano	핸드폰	cellular phone
피우다	to smoke	햄버거	hamburger
피자	pizza	행	destined for
필요하다	to be necessary	행복하다	to be happy
하고	1. and (with nouns); 2. with	헤드폰	headphones
		헤어지다	to break up
하나	one	현관	(front) entrance
하나도	(not) at all	현금	cash
하늘	sky	현재	the present
하늘색	sky blue	형	the older brother of a male
하다	to do		
하루	(one) day	형님 *hon.*	the older brother of a male
하루 종일	all day		
하숙방	a room in a boardinghouse	형제	sibling(s)
		호박	pumpkin, squash

호선	subway line
호주	Australia
호텔	hotel
혹시	by any chance
혼나다	to have a hard time
혼자	alone
홍콩	Hong Kong
화랑	gallery
화려하다	to be fancy, colorful
화면	screen
화씨	Fahrenheit
화요일	Tuesday
화장실	bathroom, restroom
화장품	cosmetics
환승	transfer
환승하다	to transfer (a ride)
회사	company
횡단보도	crosswalk
후	after
후추	black pepper
휴게실	lounge
휴일	holiday, day off
휴지	toilet paper
흐려지다	to get cloudy
흐리다	to be cloudy
흰색	white
힘(이) 들다	to be hard

English - Korean Glossary

0 (zero)	영	alone	혼자
0 (zero)	공 (phone #)	already	벌써
1	일	also, too	도
2	이	alteration	수선
3	삼	always	항상
4	사	a.m.	오전
about	에 대해서	a moment ago	방금
about, around	쯤	and	그리고
academic term	학기	and (joins nouns)	와/과
accessories	액세서리		하고
accident	사고	and, also, too	또
according to	에 따라	animal (counter)	마리
account	계좌	answer	답
action	액션		대답
A.D.	서기	answer [to]	대답하다
adapt [to]	적응하다	answering machine	자동 응답기
adaptation	적응	antique	골동품
address	주소	a pair of (counter)	벌
adult, (one's) elders	어른	apartment	아파트
a few days	며칠	appetite	식성
after	후	apple	사과
after a long time	오래간만	appoint [to]	지정하다
afternoon	오후	approximate	정도
again	다시	approximately	약
age	나이 *plain*	architecture	건축학
	연세 *hon.*	area code	지역 번호
air	공기	arrange [to]	정리하다
air conditioner	에어컨	arrive [to]	도착하다
airfare	항공료	art	예술
airplane	비행기	articles, goods	물품
airport	공항	Asia	아시아
aisle	복도	Asian studies	동양학
Alaska	알래스카	ask [to]	묻다
alcoholic beverage	술	ask a favor [to]	부탁하다
Alien Registration	외국인등록	at, in, on (time)	에
number	번호	at all [not]	하나도
a little	조금	at least	적어도
	좀	attend [to]	다니다
a little later	이따가	Australia	호주
all	다	automatically	저절로
	모두	automobile	자동차
all day	하루 종일	autumn, fall	가을
all together	전부	a while ago	아까
almost	거의	back, behind	뒤

bag	가방	be closed [to]	닫히다
bakery	제과점	be cloudy [to]	흐리다
ballpoint pen	볼펜	be cold [to]	차다
bank	은행		춥다
barber shop	이발소	become [to]	되다
bargain sale	바겐 세일	become cooler [to]	시원해지다
baseball	야구	be comfortable [to]	편안하다
baseball stadium	야구장		편하다
basketball	농구	be convenient [to]	편리하다
basketball game	농구 시합	be cool, refreshing [to]	시원하다
bath	목욕	be correct [to]	맞다
bathe [to]	목욕하다	be crowded [to]	복잡하다
bathroom, restroom	화장실	bed	침대
battery	배터리	be dangerous [to]	위험하다
B.C.	기원전	be dark [to]	어둡다
be (equation) [to]	이다	be delicious [to]	맛있다
be (existence) [to]	있다	be deprived of [to]	뺏기다
be (existence), stay [to]	계시다hon.	be different [to]	다르다
be accurate [to]	정확하다	be difficult [to]	어렵다
beach	바닷가	be dirty [to]	더럽다
be all right, okay [to]	괜찮다	be diverse [to]	다양하다
be amazing [to]	신기하다	bedroom	침실
bean sprout	콩나물	be dry [to]	건조하다
beauty salon	미용실	be easy [to]	쉽다
be bad [to]	나쁘다	beef	소고기
be beautiful [to]	아름답다	be excited [to]	신나다
be big [to]	크다	be excused [to]	실례하다
be bitten [to]	물리다	be expensive [to]	비싸다
be bitter [to]	쓰다	be familiar [to]	익숙하다
be black [to]	까맣다	be famous [to]	유명하다
be bland [to]	싱겁다	be fancy, colorful [to]	화려하다
be blocked [to]	막히다	be far [to]	멀다
be blue [to]	파랗다	be fast [to]	빠르다
be bored [to]	심심하다	be fat [to]	뚱뚱하다
be boring [to]	지겹다	be few, scarce [to]	적다
be born [to]	태어나다	be foggy [to]	끼다
be bright [to]	밝다	before	전
be busy [to]	바쁘다	be formed [to]	생기다
be careful [to]	조심하다	begin [to]	시작하다
be caught [to]	잡히다	be glad [to]	반갑다
because of	때문에	be good, nice [to]	좋다
be changed [to]	바뀌다	be good-natured [to]	착하다
be cheap [to]	싸다	be handsome [to]	잘생기다
be clean [to]	깨끗하다	be happy [to]	행복하다
be clear [to]	맑다	be hard [to]	힘(이) 들다
be close (to) [to]	친하다	be healthy [to]	건강하다
be close, near [to]	가깝다	be heavy [to]	무겁다

be high [to]	높다	be small (in size) [to]	작다
be hot [to]	덥다		조그맣다
	뜨겁다	be so [to]	그렇다
be hot and humid [to]	무덥다	be sold [to]	팔리다
be how [to]	어떻다	be sorry [to]	미안하다
be hungry [to]	배(가)		죄송하다
	고프다	be sour [to]	시다
be identical [to]	똑같다	be spacious, wide [to]	넓다
be important [to]	중요하다	be special [to]	특별하다
be in fashion [to]	유행하다	be spicy [to]	맵다
be insufficient [to]	부족하다	be stylish, attractive [to]	멋있다
be interesting, fun [to]	재미있다	be surprised [to]	놀라다
be joyful [to]	즐겁다	be sweet [to]	달다
be joyful, glad [to]	기쁘다	be tall in height [to]	키가 크다
be kind, considerate [to]	친절하다	be tasteless [to]	맛없다
be late [to]	늦다	be thankful [to]	감사하다
be light [to]	가볍다		고맙다
be lonely [to]	외롭다	be thick [to]	두껍다
be long [to]	길다	be thin [to]	얇다
be low [to]	낮다	be thirsty [to]	목(이)
below the freezing point	영하		마르다
be many, much [to]	많다	be tired [to]	피곤하다
be narrow [to]	좁다	be to one's liking [to]	마음에 들다
be neat [to]	단정하다	between	사이
be necessary [to]	필요하다	between, among	중에서
be noisy [to]	시끄럽다	be ugly [to]	못생기다
be open [to]	열리다	be uncomfortable [to]	불편하다
be over, finished [to]	끝나다	be undesirable [to]	싫다
be passive [to]	소극적이다	be uninteresting [to]	재미없다
be positive [to]	적극적이다	be used [to]	쓰이다
be pretty [to]	예쁘다	beverage	음료수
be quiet [to]	조용하다	be warm [to]	따뜻하다
be red [to]	빨갛다		포근하다
be sad [to]	슬프다	be well [to]	안녕하다
	아쉽다	be white [to]	하얗다
be safe [to]	안전하다	be wished [to]	기다려지다
be salty [to]	짜다	be yellow [to]	노랗다
be scary, scared [to]	무섭다	be young [to]	어리다
be seen, visible [to]	보이다	bicycle	자전거
be short [to]	짧다	biology	생물학
be short in height [to]	키가 작다	birthday	생일 *plain*
be sick [to]	아프다		생신 *hon.*
be similar [to]	비슷하다	bite [to]	물다
be skinny [to]	마르다	black	검정 색
be sleepy [to]	졸리다	black (=까망)	까만색
be slim [to]	날씬하다	blackboard	칠판

black pepper	후추
bloom [to]	피다
blouse	블라우스
blow [to]	불다
blue	파란색
blue jeans	청바지
boarding expenses	하숙비
boarding house	하숙집
body	몸
boil [to]	끓다
	끓이다
book	책
bookshelf, bookcase	책장
bookstore	책방
	서점
boots	장화
borrow [to]	빌리다
Boston	보스톤
bottom [the], below	밑
bowling	볼링
box	박스
	상자
bread	빵
break [to]	깨지다
break down [to]	고장나다
breakdown	고장
breakfast	아침
break up [to]	헤어지다
bring [to]	갖고 오다
bring and put down somewhere [to]	갖다 놓다
bring/take something to someone [to]	갖다 드리다
bring/take something to someone [to]	갖다 주다
broadcasting station	방송국
Broadway theater	브로드웨이 극장
brush one's teeth [to]	이(를) 닦다
Buddhism	불교
Buddhist temple	절
building	건물
	빌딩
building, structure	건축물
Bulguksa	불국사
bundle, bunch (counter)	단
bus	버스

but, however	그런데
	그렇지만
butcher shop	정육점
buy [to]	사다
buy and eat [to]	사 먹다
buy one's groceries [to]	장(을) 보다
by any chance	혹시
by chance, accident	우연히
by means of	으로
by the way	그런데, 근데
	참
cable car	케이블카
cake	케이크
calendar	달력
call [to]	걸다
camera	카메라
campus	캠퍼스
Canada	캐나다
cannot	못
cap, hat	모자
capital city	수도
car	차
card	카드
care of health	몸조리
carrot	당근
carry around [to]	갖고 다니다
case	경우
cash	현금
catch, grab [to]	잡다
cellular phone	핸드폰
Celsius	섭씨
cent	센트
center [the], pivot	중심지
central districts [the]	중부 지방
Central Post Office [the]	중앙 우체국
century	세기
chair	의자
change (clothes) [to]	갈아 입다
change (money)	거스름돈
change (vehicles) [to]	갈아 타다
change, switch [to]	바꾸다
check, bill	계산서
Chicago	시카고
child	아이
China	중국
Chinese food	중식
choose, select [to]	고르다

chopsticks	젓가락	computer lab	컴퓨터 랩
Christmas	크리스마스	concert	음악회
church	교회		콘서트
cigarette	담배	condiment, seasoning	양념
city	도시	congratulate [to]	축하하다
city hall	시청	connect, link [to]	연결하다
city hall station	시청역	connection, link	연결
class	반	construction	공사
	클래스	contact	연락
classical music	클래식	contact [to]	연락하다
classroom	교실	contact lens	콘택트 렌즈
clean [to]	청소하다	contain [to]	들어있다
cleaner's	세탁소	continue [to]	계속되다
cleaning	청소	continuously	계속
clerk, salesperson	점원	convenience store	편의점
clock, watch	시계	cook [to]	요리하다
close [to]	닫다	cooked rice	밥
close, cover [to]	덮다	cooking	요리
closet	장롱	cosmetics	화장품
clothes	옷	cost money [to]	돈이 들다
clothing habits	의생활	cost of living	물가
clothing store	옷가게	country	나라
cloud	구름	course, class	수업
club	클럽	course, subject	과목
coat	코트	cracker	과자
coffee	커피	craftwork	공예품
coffee shop, café	커피숍	credit card	신용 카드
cola	콜라	cross [to]	건너다
collect [to]	모으다	crossroads, intersection	사거리
college, university	대학	cry [to]	울다
	대학교	Cuba	쿠바
college student	대학생	culture	문화
color	색, 색깔	cut [to]	자르다
come [to]	오다	cut (something for	잘라 드리다
comedy	코미디	someone) [to]	
come/go riding [to]	타고 다니다	cut (something	잘라 주다 *plain*
come in [to]	들어오다	for someone) [to]	
come on foot [to]	걸어오다	cut down [to]	깎다
come out [to]	나오다	Dabo Tower	다보탑
come out to greet	마중 나오다	daily life, living	생활
someone [to]		dance	춤
come riding [to]	타고 오다	dance [to]	춤(을) 추다
comic book	만화책	date	날짜
comic book rental store	만화방		데이트
commencement	졸업식	date [to]	데이트하다
company	회사		사귀다
computer	컴퓨터	date of birth	생년월일

daughter	딸*plain*	downstairs	아래층
	따님*hon.*	downtown	시내
dawn	새벽	doze off [to]	졸다
day	날	drama	드라마
day (counter)	일	draw [to]	그리다
day [one]	하루	drawer	서랍
day after tomorrow [the]	모레	dream a dream [to]	꿈(을) 꾸다
daytime	낮	dress [one-piece]	원피스
degree	도	dress shirt	와이셔츠
deliver [to]	배달하다	dress shoes	구두
delivery	배달	drink [to]	마시다
delivery service	택배	drive [to]	운전하다
depart [to]	출발하다	driver	기사
department store	백화점	driver's license	운전 면허
departure	출발	driving	운전
desk	책상	drugstore	약국
destined for	행	drum	드럼
develop, grow [to]	발달하다	during	동안
development	발달	each	각
dialect	사투리	each other	서로
dictionary	사전	early	일찍
die [to]	죽다	earn (money) [to]	벌다
digit	자리	earn money [to]	돈을 벌다
diligently	열심히	earring	귀걸이
dining table	식탁	east	동
dinner	저녁	East Coast	동부
directly	바로	East Hall	이스트 홀
	직접	eat [to]	드시다*hon.*
disappear [to]	없어지다		먹다*plain*
discount	할인	eat out [to]	외식하다
dish	그릇	economics	경제학
dishwashing	설거지	economy-class seat	일반석
dishwashing [to do]	설거지하다	education	교육학
dislike [to]	싫어하다	egg	계란
distance	거리	electrical engineering	전기공학
do [to]	하다	elementary school	초등학교
doctor	의사	elementary school	초등학생
dog	개	student	
do homework [to]	숙제하다	elevator	엘리베이터
dollar	달러	e-mail	이메일
	불	employee	종업원
do not	안	engagement	약속
do the laundry [to]	빨래하다	English language [the]	영어
domestic flight	국내선	enjoy [to]	즐기다
Dongdaemun Market	동대문시장	enter [to]	들어가다
door	문	entrance	입구
dormitory	기숙사	entrance [front]	현관

envelope	봉투	floor	바닥
et cetera	등	floor, layer (counter)	층
Europe	유럽	floor heating system	온돌
evening	저녁	flower	꽃
event	일	flower shop	꽃집
every day	날마다	fog	안개
	매일	food	음식
every month	매달	food cost	음식값
every week	매주	food expenses	식비
every year	매년	foot	발
exercise	연습 문제	football	풋볼
	운동	for, per	에
exercise [to]	운동하다	for a long time	오랫동안
exit	출구	for a short time	잠깐만
experience	경험	foreign country	외국
eyeglasses	안경	foreign language	외국어
eyes	눈	foreigner	외국인
face	얼굴	for example	예를 들어
fact, truth	사실	forget [to]	잊다
factory	공장	four days	나흘
Fahrenheit	화씨	France	프랑스
fall (down) [to]	넘어지다	free of charge	무료
fall asleep [to]	잠이 들다	freeze [to]	얼다
fall foliage	단풍	freshman	1학년
family	가족	Friday	금요일
fare (bus, taxi)	차비	friend	친구
farming	농사	from (a person or	한테서
fashion, trend	유행	an animal)	
fast, quickly	빨리	from (location)	에서
father	아버지	from (time)	에서
feast, party	잔치	from (time) . . .	부터
fee, fare	요금	from next time	다음부터(는)
feeling	기분	front [the]	앞
fight [to]	싸우다	fruit	과일
find, look for [to]	찾다	function, work [to]	되다
find out, check out [to]	알아보다	furniture	가구
fire station	소방서	furniture store	가구점
first	첫	gain age [to]	나이가 들다
first, beforehand	먼저	gallery	화랑
first, most	제일	game	게임
first birthday [the]	돌	game, match	시합
first-class seat	일등석	Gangwon region	강원
first-time [the]	처음	garage	차고
fish	생선	garlic	마늘
fishery	어업	gas station	주유소
fit [to]	맞다	gather [to]	모이다
flesh, fat	살	generally, mostly	대체로

English	Korean
get, turn into [to]	되다
get along [to]	지내다
get around [to]	다니다
get busier [to]	바빠지다
get cloudy [to]	구름이 끼다
	흐려지다
get colder [to]	추워지다
get in/on, ride [to]	타다
get lower [to]	낮아지다
get married [to]	결혼하다
get off [to]	내리다
get up [to]	일어나다
girlfriend	여자 친구
give [to]	드리다*hum.*
	주다*plain*
give a present, gift [to]	선물하다
glass, cup	잔
gloves	장갑
go [to]	가다
go and get back [to]	다녀 오다
go down (the Sun) [to]	지다
go down [to]	내려가다
gold ring	금반지
golf	골프
good fortune	복
go on foot [to]	걸어가다
go out [to]	나가다
go out to greet someone [to]	마중 나가다
go riding [to]	타고 가다
go up [to]	올라가다
grade	성적
gradually	차차
graduate [to]	졸업하다
graduate school	대학원
graduate student	대학원생
graduation	졸업
gram	그램
grandfather	할아버지
grandmother	할머니
green	초록색
green tea	녹차
greet [to]	인사하다
greeting	인사
grow up [to]	자라다
guard, protect [to]	지키다
guest, customer	손님
guitar	기타
Gwanak Mountain	관악산
Gyeongju	경주
hair	머리
half	반
half price	반값
Halla Mount	한라산
hamburger	햄버거
hand	손
Hangeul Day	한글날
happen, break out	[noun] 나다
hardship	고생
have [to]	있다
have, catch a cold [to]	감기에 걸리다
have a difficult time [to]	고생하다
have a full stomach [to]	배(가) 부르다
have a hard time [to]	혼나다
have a meal [to]	식사하다
Hawai`i	하와이
head	머리
headphones	헤드폰
heat [to]	달구다
heating	난방
heel	굽
height	키
hello (on the phone)	여보세요
help	도움
help [to]	돕다
	도와 주다*pl*
	도와 드리다*h*
here	여기
highest [the]	최고
high-rise building	고층빌딩
high school	고등학교
high school student	고등학생
highway, freeway	고속도로
hike [to]	등산하다
hiking	등산
history	역사
hobby	취미
holiday, day off	휴일
home, house	집*plain*
	댁*hon.*
hometown	고향
homework	숙제

honey, dear	여보	*japchae*	잡채
Hong Kong	홍콩	jazz	재즈
horror movie	공포 영화	Jeju Island	제주도
hospital	병원	journal	일기
hotel	호텔	juice	주스
hot shredded-beef soup	육개장	jumper/jacket	점퍼
hour, o'clock	시	junior	3학년
how	어떻게	just, just in time	마침
how long/much	얼마	just, without any special	그냥
how long/much	얼마나	reason	
how many, what	몇	*kalbi* (spareribs)	갈비
(with a counter)		karaoke room	노래방
hurry [to]	서두르다	key	열쇠
hurt [to]	다치다	kimchi	김치
I	나 *plain*	*kimpab*	김밥
	저 *hum.*	kitchen	부엌
ice	얼음	know [to]	알다
ice cream	아이스크림	Korea	한국
ice hockey	아이스하키	Korea town	한인타운
identification card	신분증	Korean airline	대한항공
improve [to]	늘다	Korean alphabet	한글
in, at (dynamic location)	에서	Korean dry sauna	찜질방
in, at, on (static location)	에	Korean language	한국말
Incheon	인천		한국어
including	까지	Korean studies	한국학
inform [to]	알리다	Korean food	한식
in peace	안녕히	lab	랩
inquire [to]	물어보다	lack [to]	모자라다
Insadong	인사동	lamp	램프
inside [the]	안	last, past	지난
instant noodles (ramen)	라면	last night	어젯밤
international call	국제 전화	last year	작년
international flight	국제선	late	늦게
Internet	인터넷	later	나중에
Internet café	피시방	laugh [to]	웃다
intersection, crossroads	네거리	law	법학
interview	인터뷰	learn [to]	배우다
introduce [to]	소개하다	leave (a message) [to]	남기다
introduction	소개	leave [to]	떠나다
I see	네	left side	왼쪽
island	섬	lend [to]	빌려주다
Italy	이태리	less	덜
item (counter)	개	lesson, chapter	과
jacket	자켓	letter	편지
Jamsil	잠실	lettuce	상추
Japan	일본	library	도서관
Japanese food	일식	lie down [to]	눕다

like [to]	좋아하다	meal	밥
linguistics	언어학		식사
listen [to]	듣다	mean, signify [to]	뜻하다
literature	문학	meantime	그동안
live [to]	살다	meat	고기
live on one's own [to]	자취하다	mechanical engineering	기계 공학
living on one's own	자취	medicine	약
living room	거실	meet [to]	만나다
London	런던	memorable	인상적
long-distance call	장거리 전화	memorize [to]	외우다
long time	오래	memory	기억
look around,	구경하다	menu	메뉴
sightsee [to]		merchandise, stuff	물건
Los Angeles (L.A.)	로스	message	메시지
	앤젤레스	meter	미터기
lose [to]	잃어버리다	Mexico	멕시코
lose, be defeated [to]	지다	middle [the]	중간
loud(ly)	크게	middle, center [the]	가운데
lounge	휴게실	middle-aged woman	아주머니
	라운지	middle school	중학교
love	사랑	middle school student	중학생
love [to]	사랑하다	milk	우유
lowest [the]	최저	million	백만
luck, fortune	운	mind, heart	마음
luggage, load	짐	minute (counter)	분
lunar calendar	음력	miss, long for [to]	그립다
lunch	점심	mister	아저씨
magazine	잡지	mom	엄마
mail (a letter, parcel) [to]	부치다	Monday	월요일
mail service	우편	money	돈
main character	주인공	month (counter)	개월
major	전공		월
major [to]	전공하다		달
make [to]	만들다	moon	달
make a phone call [to]	통화하다	more	더
	전화하다	more or less	다소
make friends [to]	사귀다	morning	아침
man	남자	most [the]	가장
many, several	여러	mostly, mainly	주로
map	지도	motel	모텔
market	마켓	mother	어머니
marketplace	시장	mountain climber	등산객
marriage	결혼	move [to]	이사하다
mart	마트	move, shift [to]	옮기다
master bedroom	안방	movie	영화
match, game	경기	movie theater	극장
match, suit [to]	어울리다	much, many	많이

muffler	목도리	number of times	번
museum	박물관	object particle	을/를
music	음악	of	의
musical instrument	악기	office	사무실
musical performance	연주	office worker	직장인
my	제*hum.*	often, frequently	자주
	내*plain*	oh	아
naengmyŏn (cold	냉면		어
buckwheat noodles)		Oh! Oh my! Dear me!	어머
Nam Mountain	남산	okay	네
name	성함*hon.*	old days [the]	옛날
	이름*plain*	older brother of	오빠
national holidays	국경일	a female [the]	
nature	자연	older brother of	형
navy blue, indigo	남색	a male [the]	
nearby, vicinity	근처	older brother of	형님*hon.*
necklace	목걸이	a male [the]	
necktie	네타이	older sister of	언니
neighborhood	동네	a female [the]	
new	새	older sister of a male [the]	누나
New Year	새해	Olympics	올림픽
New York	뉴욕	one	하나
newly	새로	one (with counter)	한
news	뉴스	one portion	일 인 분
newspaper	신문	one-way trip	편도
newspaper publisher	신문사	onion	양파
next, following	다음	only	만
next year	내년	open [to]	열다
night	밤	open, unfold [to]	펴다
no	아니요	opera	오페라
noodles	면	oral exam	구두 시험
north	북	order [to]	주문하다
not be (existence) [to]	없다	order (food) [to]	시키다
not be (negative	아니다	ordinal numbers	번째
equation) [to]		(counter)	째
not have [to]	없다	other side [the]	건너편
not know [to]	모르다	outside	밖
not N1 but N2	말고	outside [the]	야외
not really	별로	oversleep	늦잠
not to be, not do [to]	않다	over there	저기
nothing but, only	밖에	owner	주인
novel	소설	pack [to]	싸다
now	지금	pack, bag	봉지
now	이젠(이제+는)	packing	포장
number	번호	page	쪽
	숫자	pair	켤레
number (counter)	번	pan	팬

pants	바지
paper	종이
parcel, package	소포
parents	부모님
park	공원
parking lot	주차장
particularly	유난히
	특히
part-time job	아르바이트
party	파티
pass away [to]	돌아가시다h
pass by [to]	지나가다
passport	여권
pay (money) [to]	돈을 내다
pear	배
pedestrian crossing	횡단보도
pen	펜
pencil	연필
people	분hon.
people (counter)	명plain
perform on a musical instrument [to]	연주하다
period	시대
person, people	사람
personality	성격
phone call	통화
photo, picture	사진
physics	물리학
piano	피아노
pibimbap	비빔밥
picture, painting	그림
pizza	피자
place, location	곳
	데
	장소
place, spot	군데
plan	계획
plan [to]	계획하다
play (piano, guitar) [to]	치다
play (tennis) [to]	치다
play (violin) [to]	켜다
play, drama	연극
play, not work [to]	놀다
play baseball [to]	야구하다
play basketball [to]	농구하다
playground	운동장
play soccer [to]	축구하다

plural particle	들
police	경찰
police station	경찰서
political science	정치학
popularity	인기
population	인구
postage	우편 요금
postal code	우편 번호
postbox	우체통
postcard	엽서
postman	우체부
post office	우체국
potato	감자
practice	연습
practice [to]	연습하다
preparation	준비
prepare [to]	준비하다
present [the]	현재
present, gift	선물
president	대통령
presidential election	대통령 선거
price	가격
	값
probably, perhaps	아마
problem	문제
professor	교수님
professor's office	연구실
program	프로
promise	약속
psychology	심리학
pub, bar	술집
public [the]	대중
pulgogi (roast meat)	불고기
pumpkin, squash	호박
put forth effort [to]	수고하다
put in [to]	넣다
put on [to]	얹다
put something down for someone [to]	놓아 주다
put something in [to]	집어넣다
question	질문
quick(ly)	어서
radio	라디오
rain	비
rain [to]	비(가) 오다
rainy season	장마

read [to]	독서하다	rock music	록
	읽다	rock-paper-scissors	가위바위보
reading	독서	room	방
really, truly	정말	room in a	하숙방
	참	boardinghouse	
receipt	영수증	roommate	룸메이트
receive [to]	받다	roughly	대충
recipe	만드는 법	rough map	약도
red	빨간색	round-trip	왕복
red-pepper paste	고추장	run [to]	뛰다
refrigerator	냉장고	Russia	러시아
regards	안부	sale	세일
region, district	지방	sandals	샌들
registered (mail)	등기	sandwich	샌드위치
regular	보통	Saturday	토요일
regular price	정가	sauna	사우나
relationship	사이	scallion	파
relatively	비교적	scarf	목도리
relieve [to]	풀다	scenery, view	경치
remain [to]	남다	scholarship	장학금
	남아있다	school	학교
remember [to]	기억하다	school uniform	교복
repeat after [to]	따라하다	school vacation	방학
reply	답장	school year	학년
reply [to]	답장하다	science	과학
resemble [to]	닮다	screen	화면
reservation	예약	sea	바다
reserve [to]	예약하다	search for [to]	구하다
Resident Registration	주민등록증	season	계절
card		season [to]	양념하다
Resident Registration	주민등록번호	seat	자리
number			좌석
rest [to]	쉬다	second	두 번째
restaurant	식당	see [to]	뵙다 *hum.*
	음식점	see, look, watch [to]	보다 *plain*
return (something	돌려	self-identification	본인 확인
to someone) [to]	드리다 *hum.*	sell [to]	팔다
return (something	돌려	send [to]	보내다
to someone) [to]	주다 *plain*	senior	4학년
return (to) [to]	돌아가다	Seokga Tower	석가탑
return, come back [to]	돌아오다	Seokguram (stone cave)	석굴암
review	복습	Seorak Mount	설악산
ride pass, ticket	승차권	Seoul	서울
right away, soon	곧	Seoul Tower	서울타워
right side	오른쪽	Seoul National	서울대
ring	반지	University Station	입구역
rise, come up [to]	뜨다	service	서비스

sesame oil	참기름	so, therefore	그래서
set	세트	soap	비누
sex, gender	성별	soccer	축구
shape	모양	Social Security number	사회보장
shirt	셔츠		번호
shoes	신발	socks, stockings	양말
shop [to]	쇼핑하다	sofa	소파
shopping	쇼핑	soft tofu stew	순두부찌개
shopping district	상가	solar calendar	양력
shorten [to]	줄이다	some kind of	무슨
shorts	반바지	someone	누가
show	쇼		누구
show, represent [to]	나타내다	something	뭐
shower	샤워	sometime	언제
sibling(s)	형제	sometimes	가끔
side, beside [the]	옆	somewhere	어디
side, direction	쪽	son	아들
side dishes	반찬	song	노래
sidewalk	인도	soon	금방
sightseeing	구경	sophomore	2학년
sign	표지판	sound, noise	소리
sign, signature	사인	soup	스프
Silla	신라	south	남
sincerely yours	올림	South America	남미
sing (a song) [to]	부르다	Southeast Asia	동남아
sing [to]	노래 부르다	Southern	남부
	노래하다	soybean-paste stew	된장찌개
singer	가수	soy sauce	간장
single room	독방	spaghetti	스파게티
sit [to]	앉다	Spain	스페인
size	사이즈	speak [to]	말하다
ski	스키	speech, words	말씀*hon.*
ski [to]	스키 타다		말*plain*
skirt	치마	spend time [to]	보내다
sky	하늘	spinach	시금치
sky blue	하늘색	spoon	숟가락
sleep	잠	spoons and chopsticks	수저
sleep [to]	자다*plain*	sports	스포츠
	주무시다*hon.*	sports shoes, sneakers	운동화
	잠을 자다	spread [to]	깔다
sleeve	소매	spring	봄
slice [to]	썰다	staff, employee	직원
slipper	슬리퍼	stairs	계단
slow(ly)	천천히	stamp	우표
smoke [to]	피우다	stand [to]	서다
snow	눈	star	별
snow [to]	눈(이) 오다	station	역

stick, affix [to]	붙이다	take, carry [to]	가져가다
stir-fry [to]	볶다	take a course [to]	듣다
stomach, abdomen	배	take a shower [to]	샤워하다
stop [bus]	정류장	take off, undress [to]	벗다
stop, pull over [to]	세우다	talk, chat	이야기
stop by [to]	들르다		얘기
store	가게	talk, chat [to]	이야기하다
	상점		얘기하다
store signs	간판	tangerine	귤
straight	쭉	tape	테이프
straight, upright	똑바로	taste [to]	맛보다
street, road	거리	taxi	택시
	차도	taxi fare	택시비
	길	tea	차
stress	스트레스	teach [to]	가르치다
student	학생	teacher	선생님
student abroad	유학생	teacher's wife	사모님
student center	학생회관	telephone	전화
studio apartment	원룸	telephone bill	전화비
study	공부	telephone number	전화번호
study [to]	공부하다	television	텔레비전
study room	공부방	tell, convey [to]	전하다
style	스타일	temperature	기온
subject particle	께서hon.	temple	사찰
	이/가plain	tennis	테니스
subway	지하철	tennis court	테니스장
subway line	호선	test, exam	시험
suddenly	갑자기	textbook	교과서
sugar	설탕	than	보다
suit, formal dress	정장	that	그
summer	여름	that (over there)	저
Sunday	일요일	then, in that case	그러면
supermarket	슈퍼(마켓)	then, if so	그럼
surely, certainly	꼭	there	거기
	반드시	these days	요새
sushi	스시		요즘
sweater	스웨터	thief	도둑
swim [to]	수영하다	thing	것
swimming	수영		거
swimming pool	수영장	things to eat	먹거리
Sydney	시드니	things to watch	볼거리
table	상	thinly	얇게
tablespoon	큰술	this	이
Taekwondo	태권도		이거 (=이것)
take (a photo) [to]	찍다	this time	이번
take [time] [to]	걸리다	this way	이쪽(으로)
take [to]	갖고 가다	this year	올해

thread	실	Tuesday	화요일
three days	사흘	tuition fees	학비
thriller	스릴러	turn [to]	돌다
Thursday	목요일	turn in (homework) [to]	내다
ticket	티켓 표	turn on, switch on, play (music) [to]	틀다
ticket office	매표소	two	둘
tie [to]	매다	two (with counter)	두
time	때	two days	이틀
time, hour (duration)	시간	Tylenol	타이레놀
to (a person)	한테 께 hon.	uh (expression of hesitation)	저어
to (destination)	에	umbrella	우산
to/until/through (time)	까지	uncle (father's older brother)	큰아버지
today	오늘	underground market	지하 상가
tofu	두부	underpass	지하도
together	같이	understand [to]	이해하다
together, along with	함께	understand, recognize [to]	알아듣다
toilet paper	휴지		
Tokyo	도쿄	uniform	유니폼
tomato	토마토	Union Building	유니온 빌딩
tomorrow	내일	United Kingdom [the]	영국
too much	너무	United States [the]	미국
tooth	이	up to (location)	까지
toothbrush	칫솔	use [to]	사용하다
toothpaste	치약		쓰다
topic particle ('as for')	은/는	used furniture	중고 가구
top side [the], above	위	used merchandise	중고품
toward, to	으로	usually	보통
town shuttle bus	마을 버스	utilize [to]	이용하다
tradition	전통	vacuum cleaner	청소기
traditional culture	전통 문화	Vancouver	밴쿠버
traditional holidays	명절	vegetable	야채
traditional Korean dress	한복	vending machine	발매기
traditional teahouse	전통 찻집	very, really	아주
traffic	교통	very much	굉장히
traffic light	신호등		무척
traffic sign	교통 표지판		
train	기차	violin	바이올린
transfer	환승	visa	비자
transfer (a ride) [to]	환승하다	vocabulary	단어
transportation card	교통카드	voice	목소리
travel [to]	여행하다	volume (counter)	권
travel, trip	여행	wait [to]	기다리다
travel agency	여행사	walk [to]	걷다
truck	트럭	walk around [to]	걸어다니다
T-shirt	티셔츠	wallet	지갑

want to [to]	고 싶다	wish, want [to]	원하다
wardrobe, closet	옷장	with	하고
wash dishes [to]	설거지하다	withdraw (money) [to]	찾다
washing machine	세탁기	without doing anything	그만
wash one's face [to]	세수하다	further	
wash one's hands [to]	손(을) 씻다	woman	여자
water	물	won (Korean currency)	원 (₩)
waterfall	폭포	work	일
way	길	work [to]	일하다
wealthy person	부자	World Cup	월드컵
wear, put on	입다	worry [to]	걱정하다
(clothes) [to]		worry, concern	걱정
wear (footwear) [to]	신다	worth	짜리
wear (glasses, gloves,	끼다	worth, value	어치
rings) [to]		Wow!	와
wear headgear [to]	쓰다	wrap [to]	싸다
weather	날씨	write [to]	쓰다
weather forecast	일기예보	write down [to]	적다
wedding	결혼식	yard	마당
Wednesday	수요일		정원
week	주	yeah	응 *plain*
weekend	주말	year (counter)	년
weight	무게	years old	살
well	잘	yellow	노란색
well; It's hard to say	글쎄요	yes, I see, okay	네/예
west	서	yesterday	어제
Western-style (food)	양식	yet, still	아직
we/us/our	우리 *plain*		아직도
	저희 *hum.*	you	너 *plain*
what	뭐	younger brother	남동생
	무엇	younger sibling	동생
what, what kind of	무슨	younger sister	여동생
what date	며칠	youngest child	막내
what matter	웬일	Youngseo region	영서
what place, where	어디	zoo	동물원
when	언제		
which	어느		
which, what kind of	어떤		
white	흰색		
who	누구		
who	누가(누구+가)		
whole world [the]	전세계		
why	왜		
win [to]	이기다		
wind	바람		
window seat	창가 좌석		
winter	겨울		